SPANISH FOR BEGINNERS

A Practical Guide To Learn The Basics of Spanish in 10 Days

MANUEL DE CORTES

TABLE OF CONTENTS

INTRODUCTION

Dear reader,

I firstly want to express my thanks to you for buying and downloading the book *"Spanish For Beginners: A pratical guide to learn the basics of Spanish in 10 days!"*.

I also want to tell you that you're awesome for wanting to learn this beautiful and extraordinary language. This book contains proven steps and strategies on how to communicate using the basics of the Spanish language.

Divided into 10 chapters (one chapter per day), this book is designed to provide a step by step learning guide on Spanish grammar, vocabulary, and pronunciation. Plus, it features a series of useful common everyday expressions.

This book is written in a conversational style that's easy to follow and understand. After reading this book, you'll never have to say *"No hablo Español"* ever again!

Thanks again for purchasing this book,
I hope you enjoy it!
Manuel De Cortes

CHAPTER 1:
THE SPANISH ALPHABET
(EL ALFABETO ESPAÑOL)

Spanish is one of the most frequently spoken languages of today. It is also one of the easiest ones to learn for English-speaking people since its alphabet is very similar to the alphabets of other European languages.

In order to learn to speak Spanish, you'll have to be familiar with all the letters in the Spanish Alphabet and pronounce them all properly. Remember, letters are the building blocks for words. Each phoneme (sound represented by a symbol) should be uttered correctly in order to achieve proper pronunciation of words.

The Spanish Alphabet is composed of 30 letters. All of them are similar to the letters in the English alphabet (which contains 26 letters) plus it includes four more, namely: **ch***(che)*, **ll** *(elle)*, **rr** *(erre)*, and of course the famed **ñ** (enye).

There may be a few regional variations and such letters as **c** and **ch** may sometimes be considered as one letter. But the list of letters in the Spanish Alphabet below consist of what is most commonly taught to Spanish learners and is based on the standard Castilian Spanish.

A: a
B: be (or "grande be")
C: ce
Ch: che
D: de
E: e
F: efe

G: ge
H: hache
I: i
J: jota
K: ka
L: ele
Ll: elle

M: eme
N: ene
Ñ: eñe (pronounced "enye")
O: o
P: pe
Q: cu
R: ere
Rr: erre
S: ese

T: te
U: u
V: uve (also called "ve" or "chica ve")
W: uve doble (or doble ve)
X: equis
Y: y griega
Z: zeta (pronounced "theta)

There have been also been disagreements on whether the letters **W** and **K** should be considered as parts of the alphabet. This is because these letters are only used for words of foreign origin. Nevertheless, it's better to assume that they are included since it would make us more precise with our pronunciation guide.

On Vowels and Consonants

Have you ever noticed how some native Spanish speakers usually sound like they're mumbling? This is because Spanish consonant sounds are usually softer and less distinct than their English counterparts (with the exception of **r** and **rr**). Conversely, their vowels have more distinct sounds than their English equivalents.

Below is a guide to the proper pronunciation of vowels and consonants. Those not included are pronounced the same as their English counterparts.

- The letters **B** and **V** pose spelling problems in Spanish. They are pronounced EXACTLY THE SAME WAY. Thus the phrases "grande be" (big b) and "chica ve" (small v) in order to tell them apart. The thing is, the English sound "v" in "victory" does not exist in Spanish. **B** and **V** are usually pronounced somewhat similar to the

English "v" with one distinctive difference. That is, it is made by making the lips touch each other instead of the upper teeth and lower lip. However, there are instances when **B** and **V** are pronounced like the English "b". This happens when they are found in the beginning of a sentence or phrase.

- **C** sounds like that in "cereal" when it comes before an *e*or an *i,* and is pronounced like the "c" in "car" if otherwise. (E.g. hacer, crimen)
- **Ch** is pronounced the same as "ch" in **church**. (E.g. *Chile, muchisimas)*
- **G** is pronounced as that in "go", except when it precedes the letters *i*ore, in which case it is pronounced as the Spanish "j". (E.g. gritar, mágico)
- **H** in Spanish is always silent. (E.g. *hermano, hacienda*)
- The Spanish **J** on the other hand, does not exist in English. It sounds more like the "ch" in the foreign word *"loch"*.If you're familiar with German, know that this one sounds like the German "ch" as in *Kirche.*
- **L** is always pronounced like the first "l" in "little". (E.g. pastel)
- **Ll** on the other hand, sounds like the "y" in "yellow". Although in parts of Spain it may be pronounced like "ll" in "million" and like the "zh" sound in "azure" in parts of Latin America.
- **N** is another tricky letter. It is pronounced in three different ways, depending on where it is located in a word or sentence.
  - o Normally, it is read like the "n" in "nice". But there's a little difference, though. For Spanish speakers, the tongue is slightly farther forward. OK, here's how: try saying the English word "dance". Then try saying it again, only this time, when you pronounce the "n", try placing your tongue beneath your upper teeth (instead of near the top of the mouth, as is the case in English). See the difference?

8

- o Next is when the letter **n** is followed by the letters *b*, *v*, *f*, *m*, or *p* in which case it is pronounced like the "m" in "empathy". This applies even when such letters are not found in the same word. As in a phrase or sentence, for instance. Thus, the phrase **con permiso** is pronounced **compermiso.**
  - o Thirdly, when **n** is followed by *k* or *g*sounds, it is pronounced like the letter "k". An example is **banco** which is pronounced like the English "bank" plus o.
- **Ñ** sounds like a combination of "n" and "y" or "ni", as in *mañana* (pronounced "manyana" or "maniana")
- **P** is pronounced as that in "spot" and NOT like the strong "p" in "pot"
(E.g. padre, poco)
- **Q** sounds the same sa "k" in English. Note also that the "u" that follows immediately after it is not pronounced. (E.g. *quinse, quetzal)*
- **R** and **Rr** are pronounced by trilling the tongue at the top of the mouth
- **T,** like P, is pronounced like the "t" in "stop" and NOT like the strong "t" in "top"

  (E.g. *taco, todo*)
- **Y** is a special case. It can be used as either a vowel or a consonant. When used as vowel, it is pronounced the same as the Spanish "i". As consonant, it has the same sound as the English y.
- **Z** is pronounced like the "th" in "thin". (E.g. zeta, vez)

And speaking of vowels, the letter **A** is pronounced the same as the "a" in "father". Examples are: *madre, mapa*

The letter **I** (sometimes called *i Latina*, as distinguished from *y Griega)* is pronounced like the "ee" sound in English, such as the "e" in "me". (E.g. timbre)

O is pronounced like the "o" in "bone" although the duration in shorter. (E.g. amo, teléfono)

E usually sounds like the "e" in "met" when it is found in the beginning or in the middle of a word. When it is found at the end, it sounds more like the "é" in "café", but shorter. (E.g. enero, compadre)

U in Spanish is NEVER pronounced like the "u" in "university". It sounds more like the long "oo" in English, as in "loot". (E.g. unidos, reunión)

Diphthongs

When two letters (esp. vowels) blend together, they form a new sound. This is the case in Spanish as in English. For example, when *u* is followed by any other vowel, the sound created is that of the English "w" as in "cuaderno" and "cuerpo". The *i* when followed by any other vowel makes the "y" sound in "yellow", such as "hierba" and "bien". The combination of "*a*" and "*i*" on the other hand, is pronounced like "eye".

CHAPTER 2:
SALUDOS Y EXPRESIONES (GREETINGS & EXPRESSIONS)

Now that you know how to pronounce each individual phoneme (sound) in the Spanish Alphabet, it's time to familiarize yourself with some of the most common Spanish expressions used in everyday conversations. These expressions will come in quite a handy if you're planning to go on a trip to any Spanish-speaking country. There may be quite a few regional variations from one place to another but as a foreigner, you'll be pretty much excused and understood.

Remember that **H** is always silent and **Z** is pronounced like "th".

- Hola (Ola!) — Hi, Hello
- Buenos Dias — Good Morning (Can Also Mean "Hello!")
- Buenos Tardes — Good Afternoon
- Buenas Noches — Good Evening/Good Night
- ¿Cómo Está Usted? (Formal)/ ¿Cómo Estás? (Coloquial) — How Are You?
- Estoy/ (Muy) Bien — I'm (Very) Good.
- (Muchísimas) Gracias — Thank You (So Much)
- Muy Bien, Gracias — Very Well, Thank You.
- ¿Qué Hubo? ¿Qué Onda? — How's It Going?
- ¿Qué Pasa? — What's Happening? /What's Going On?

  ¿Cómo Te Llamas? / — What's Your Name?
  ¿Cómo Se Llama Usted? (Literally, What Are You Called?)
- Me Llamo... — I am (*your name*)

- Me Nombre es...   My name is (*your name)
- ¿Cómo se deletrea tu nombre?   How do you spell your name?
- Encantado/Encantada   It's A Pleasure To Meet You.
- Bienvenido/Bienvenida   Welcome!
- *¿Donde Va Usted?*   *Where Are You Going?*
- *Voy A La Casa*   *I'm Going Home*
- *¿Qué Hora Es?*   *What Time Is It?*
- *Son Las Dos En Punto*   *It's Two O'clock Sharp*
- *Adiós*   *Goodbye*
- *¿Habla Inglés?*   *Do You Speak English?*
- Hablo (Un Poco De) Español.   I Speak (A Little) Spanish.
- Repita, Por Favor   Please Repeat
- Otra Vez   One More Time
- Más Despacio   More Slowly
- No Comprendo   I Do Not Understand.
- Por Favor   Please
- De Nada   You're Welcome
- No Hay De Qué   It Was My Pleasure
- Con Permiso   Excuse Me
- Lo Siento (Mucho)   I'm (Very) Sorry
- Señor   Sir, Mr.
- Señora   Ma'am, Mrs.
- Señorita   Miss
- Tengo Una Pregunta   I Have a Problem.
- *¿Como?*   *What?*
- *Sí*   *Yes*
- *No*   *No*
- *Hay*   *There is/are*
- *Hay mas*   *There is/are more*
- *¿Cómo Se Dice _ En Español?*   *How Do You Say_ In Spanish?*
- *No Sé*   *I Don't Know.*
- *Yo Tengo Ambre*   *I'm Hungry*
- ¡Adios! ¡Chau!   Good-bye, Bye, Bye-Bye

- ¡Hasta luego! ¡Nos vemos!   So long! See you later!
- ¡Hasta pronto!   See you soon!
- ¡Hasta mañana!   See you (Till) tomorrow!
- *¡Hasta el mediodía!*   See you at noon!
- *¡Hasta la noche!*   See you in the evening (at night)!

- ¡Hasta la próxima!   Till next time!
- ¡Qué pases un lindo día!   Have a nice day!
- *No importa*   *It doesn't matter. (Never mind.)*

- *¡Felicitaciones!*   *Congratulations!*
- ¿Dónde está el baño?   Where is the bathroom?
- ¿Dónde está mi cuarto?   Where is my room?
- ¿Puedo entrar/pasar?   Can I enter/come in?
- ¿Puedo tener más, por favor?-   Can I have more, please?
- ¿Me puedes ayudar?   Can you help me?
- ¿Dónde estamos ahora?   Where are we right now?
- ¿Dónde está la calle ___?   Where is the _____street?

- ¿Me puedes prestar $5?   Can you loan me $5?
- ¿Dónde está el autobús?   Where is the bus?
- ¿Puedes guardarlo, por favor?   Can you hold this, please?
- ¿Quieres uno?   Do you want one?
- ¿Puedo tener uno?   Can I have one?
- ¿Podemos compartir?   Can we share?
- ¿Se vende _____ aquí?   Do you sell _____ here?
- ¿Cuánto cuesta?   -   How much does it cost?
- ¿Tienes cambio?   -   Do you have change?
- Que tenga un buen día!   -   I hope you have a good day!

- ¡Ten un buen día!   -   Have a good day!
- ¡Nos vemos!   We'll see each other later!
- ¡Hasta luego!   See you later!
- ¡Nos vemos al rato!   See you in a little bit!
- Nos reunimos el _____ (día).   We'll meet on _____ (day).

- Nos hablamos luego.   We'll talk later.
- Háblame.   Call me. (Talk to me)
- Llámame.   Call me.
- Fue un placer conocerte.   It was a pleasure to meet you.

Notice something different about Spanish punctuation? It's a distinctive feature of Spanish as a language. Thos inverted exclamations (¡) and question marks (¿) found at the beginning of some sentences *are not to be missed. They are an essential part of the sentence itself. In cases wherein a single statement contains more than just a question, the question marks are used to frame the interrogative statement only. For example,*

La comida es buena, ¿no es así? – The food is good, isn't it?

The same is true for exclamations found within declarative sentences.

You are bound to learn more as you go through. Remember these and soon you'll be able to form your own sentences using a few of our...

CHAPTER 3:
BASIC VOCABULARY

La Familia (The Family)

Man/Boy	Hombre/Chico	Woman/Girl	Mujer/Chica
father	padre	mother	madre
brother	hermano	sister	hermana
son	hijo	daughter	hija
baby	niño	baby	niña
husband	esposo	wife	esposa
grandfather	abuelo	grandmother	abuela
grandson	nieto	granddaughter	nieta
cousin	primo	cousin	prima
uncle	tío	aunt	tía
nephew	sobrino	niece	sobrina

Notice how the end of each word is changed from "o" to "a" depending on whether you are referring to a man or a woman. Gender is very important in Spanish and is an integral part of Spanish grammar. You will also learn that gender is not only applicable to persons. We'll have a more detailed discussion on gender in the next chapters.

Números (Numbers)

1	uno	21	veintiuno
2	dos	22	veintidós
3	tres	23	veintitrés
4	cuatro	24	veinticuatro
5	cinco	25	veinticinco
6	seis	26	veintiséis
7	siete	27	veintisiete
8	ocho	28	veintiocho
9	nueve	29	veintinueve
10	diez	30	treinta
11	once	31	treinta y uno
12	doce	32	treinta y dos
13	trece	40	cuarenta
14	catorce	41	cuarenta y uno
15	quince	42	cuarenta y dos
16	dieciséis	50	cincuenta
17	diecisiete	60	sisenta
18	dieciocho	70	setenta
19	diecinueve	80	ochenta
20	veinte	90	noventa

As you can see, there's a definite pattern when adding a digit to the end of each two-digit number onwards. For numbers 20-29, just drop the "e" at the end and replace it with "i" plus the number to be added.

For example:

- veinte + 1 = veintiuno
- veinte + 2 = veintidos and so on.

For numbers higher than 29, just write down the name of the number + y + the digit to be added.

For example:

- cuarenta + 2 = cuarenta y dos
- cincuenta + 2 = cincuenta y dos and so on.

La Hora (Time)

What time is it?	¿Qué hora es?	
It's one o'clock	Es la una.	01:00 h.
It's two o'clock	Son las dos.	02:00 h.
It's 3:30	Son las tres y media.	03:30 h.
It's 4:15	Son las cuatro y quince.	04:15 h.
It's 4:45	Son las cuatro y cuarenta y cinco.	04:45 h.
It's 6:50	Son las seis y cincuenta.	06:50 h.
It's 6am	Son las seis de la mañana.	06:00 h.
It's 3pm	Son las tres de la tarde. Son las quince.	15:00 h.
It's 6pm	Son las seis de la noche. Son las dieciocho. *(It's the 18th hour)*	18:00 h.
It's noon	Es mediodía. *(It's high noon)* Son las doce de día. *(It's 12 o'clock noon)*	12:00 h.
It's midnight	Es medianoche. *(It's midnight)* Son las doce de la noche. *(It's 12 o'clock in the evening)*	00:00 h.

Remember that there is no Spanish equivalent for **am** and **pm**. One can say ***de la mañana*** (meaning, *in the morning*), ***de la tarde*** (in the afternoon) and ***de la noche*** (in the evening). Thus, 7:00 am is ***a las siete en punto de la mañana*** (*7:00 o'clock in the morning, sharp*) and 7:00 pm is ***a las siete de la noche*** (*seven in the evening*).

Usually, the practice is to use the 24-hour system. Thus, 1:00pm would be *a las trese* (13:00 h.) Note that the words "es" and "son" translate as "it is" in English.

Los Pasatiempos (Sports & Hobbies)
Literally, Pastimes

basketball	el baloncesto
biking	el ciclismo
chess	el ajedrez
cooking	la cocina
dancing	el baile
fishing	la pesca
football	el fútbol americano
gardening	la jardinería
hiking	el excursionismo
hunting	la caza
jogging	el footing
a movie	una película
music	la música
reading	la lectura
sailing	la vela
skiing	el esquí
soccer	el fútbol
swimming	la natación
television	la televisión
tennis	el tenis
wrestling	la lucha

En la casa (In the house)

at my house	en mi casa	*kitchen*	**la** cocina
room	**el** cuarto	*dining room*	**el** comedor
hall	**el** pasillo	*bathroom*	**el** baño
stairway	**la** escalera	*office, study*	**el** despacho
porch	**la** veranda	*den, living room*	**el** salón
balcony	**el** balcón	*bedroom*	**el** dormitorio
patio	**el** patio	*basement*	**el** sótano
yard, garden	**el** jardín	*attic*	**el** desván

El Cuerpo (The human body)

hair	el pelo	**arm**	el brazo
head	la cabeza	**shoulder**	el hombro
face	la cara	**elbow**	el codo
eye	el ojo	**wrist**	la muñeca
nose	la nariz	**hand**	la mano
cheek	la mejilla	**finger**	el dedo
mouth	la boca	**fingernail**	la uña
lip	el labio	**thumb**	el pulgar
tooth	el diente	**leg**	la pierna
ear	la oreja	**knee**	la rodilla
neck	el cuello	**ankle**	el tobillo
chest	el pecho	**foot**	el pie
back	la espalda	**toe**	el dedo del pie
stomach	el estómago		

Los Colores (Colours)

	Masculine	Feminine
red	rojo**/s**	**roja/s**
purple	violeta**/s**	**violeta/s**
blue	azul**/es**	**azul/es**
green	verde**/s**	**verde/s**
yellow	amarillo**/s**	**amarilla/s**
orange	anaranjado**/s**	**anaranjada/s**
black	negro**/s**	**negra/s**
white	blanco**/s**	**blanca/s**
grey	gris**/es**	**gris/es**
brown	marrón**/es**	**marrón/es**
pink	rosado**/s**	**rosada/s**

Los Alimentos (Food)

tener hambre	to be hungry	**el** bocadillo	snack
comer	to eat	**el** aperitivo	appetizer
tener sed	to be thirsty	**la** sopa	soup
beber, tomar	to drink	**el** plato principal	main course
la comida	meal	**la** ensalada	salad
el desayuno	breakfast	**el** postre	dessert
el almuerzo	lunch	**la** cocina	kitchen, cooking
la cena	dinner	**el** comedor	dining room

Ropa (Clothing)

un abrigo	coat
un impermeable	raincoat
una chaqueta	jacket
un suéter	sweater
una camiseta	T-shirt
unos pantalones	pants
unos pantalones cortos	shorts
un traje de baño	bathing suit
unos calcetines	socks
unos zapatos	shoes
unos deportivos	sneakers
unas botas	boots
unas sandalias	sandals
un pijama	pajamas
los guantes	gloves
el cierre	zipper
el vestido	dress
la agujeta	shoelace

El Calendario (The Calendar)

LOS DÍAS DE LA SEMANA	DAYS OF THE WEEK
lunes	Monday
martes	Tuesday
miércoles	Wednesday
jueves	Thursday
viernes	Friday
sábado	Saturday
domingo	Sunday
LAS ESTACIONES	SEASONS
la primavera	spring
el verano	summer

el otoño	autumn
el invierno	winter

LOS MESES DEL AÑO	MONTHS OF THE YEAR
enero	January
febrero	February
marzo	March
abril	April
mayo	May
junio	June
julio	July
agosto	August
septiembre	September
octubre	October
noviembre	November
diciembre	December

Note: The names of days, months and seasons are NOT capitalized in Spanish. (Capitalization will be discussed in Chapter 5)

Las Plantas (Plants)

el árbol	tree	**la rosa**	rose
el tallo	stem	**la margarita**	daisy
la enredadera	vine	**la violeta**	violet
la flor	flower	**la orquídea**	orchid
la hoja	leaf	**el tulipán**	tulip
el arbusto	bush	**el cactus**	cactus
el bulbo	bulb	**el botón**	bud

Los Trabajos (Professions)

actor/ actress	**un actor/una actriz**
artist	un/a artista
baker	panadero
butcher	carnicero
carpenter	carpintero
cashier	cajero
civil servant	funcionario
cook	cocinero
doctor	médico
electrician	un/a electricista
employee	empleado
engineer	ingeniero
flight attendant	un(a) auxiliar de vuelo
lawyer (barrister)	abogado
maid	una criada
manager	director
mechanic	mecánico
nurse	enfermero
pilot	el piloto
plumber	un plomero
police officer	un policía
receptionist	una recepcionista
secretary	secretario
student	un/a estudiante
teacher	profesor
waiter/waitress	camarero
writer	escritor

El Tiempo (The Weather)

hace sol	it's sunny
el sol	the sun
frio	cold
calor	hot
hace viento	it's windy
ventoso	windy
la nube	the cloud
nublado	cloudy
la lluvia	the rain
el huracán	the hurricane
la neblina	the fog
nebuloso	foggy
el inundación de agua	the flood
el tornado	the tornado
la nieve	the snow

Los Animales(Animals)

la abeja	bee
al león	lion
la araña	spider
el burro	donkey
el alacrán	scorpion
el alce	moose
la mariposa	butterfly
la lechuza, la búho	owl
la mosca	fly
la cucaracha	cockroach
el gato	cat
el cuervo	crow
el escarabajo	beetle
el halcón	hawk

la hormiga	ant
el grillo	cricket
el zorro	fox
la víbora	snake
el gorrión	sparrow
el cisne	swan
el conejo	rabbit
el cocodrilo	crocodile
la oveja	sheep
el saltamontes	grasshopper
el tiburón	shark
el zancudo	mosquito
la rana	frog
el perro	dog
el caimán	alligator
el oso	bear

Common Objects

la manta	blanket
la botella	bottle
la caja	box
la taza	cup
la sarten	frying pan
la llave	key
el papel	paper
el cuchillo	knife
la cerradura	padlock
la almohada	pillow
el boligrafo	ballpoint pen
el lapiz	pencil
las tijeras	scissors
la pala	shovel
la grapadora	stapler

el abrelatas	can opener
la carretilla	wheelbarrow
la cacerola	saucepan
la maquinilla de afeitar	razor
el vaso	glass

Right now you probably have one thing in mind: *"How on earth am I supposed to memorize all that?"* Fortunately, the answer is you don't have to. You'll encounter these words several times as we go through. Also, if you expose yourself to the language often, you are likely to hear several terms or phrases over and over and become familiar with them. So all you have to do is go over this once or twice and you'll be fine. There's no need to worry about committing everything to memory.

Also, learning new words becomes more efficient when we use them in sentences. This way, we are less likely to forget the new words that we learn. But before you do, you'll first have to be familiar with the other nuances of the Spanish language, especially on the rules regarding number and gender. This way, you'll avoid being misunderstood. Since Spanish is both number and gender sensitive, getting one of these elements wrong can make you convey a different meaning than what you actually intended so you'll have to be very careful.

CHAPTER 4:
SPANISH PLURALS

Forming plurals in Spanish is easy. That's because it is very similar to how plurals are formed in English. As a general rule, there are three things to remember when making nouns, pronouns and adjectives plural:

1. For words that end in a vowel, simply add "s".

    Examples:un taco (a taco), dos tacos (two tacos)
    un perro (a dog), dos perros (two dogs)
    This goes as a general rule. However, when we're dealing with stressed vowels, only words ending with the stressed *–é forms a plural by simply adding "s". Other stressed vowels have an "es" added to form their plurals.*
    ***Examples**: el café (the coffee), los cafés (the coffees)*
    el rubí (the ruby), los rubies (the rubies)
    BUT, there are also exceptions, namely:
    una mamá (a mother), *tres mamás* (three mothers), *el papá* (the father), *los papás* (the fathers), *un sofá* (a sofa), *dos sofás* (two sofas) and *el dominó* (the domino), *los dominós* (the dominoes)
2. For words ending in consonants, add "es"
    Examples: un árbol (a tree), tres arboles (three trees)
    el actor (the actor), los actores (the actors)
    For pluralization purposes, *y*is considered a consonant.
3. Finally, the third rule is: for words ending in **z,** change **z** to **c** and add "es"
    Examples: una vez (once), dos veces (twice)
    voz (voice), voz (voices)

CHAPTER 5:
GENDER

Gender is considered an inherent trait of Spanish nouns and adjectives, with only a few exceptions. This means that even inanimate objects in Spanish have genders.

This is the principal difference between the concept of *sex* and *gender* in Spanish. Sex refers to a person or animal's being male or female. Gender, on the other hand, is more encompassing.

Any person who wishes to speak Spanish correctly should be familiar with the rules governing gender since it determines which pronouns we should use with the nouns and how they are incorporated in a phrase or sentence.

The Gender of Nouns

To make things easier, do not confuse gender with sex. Think of gender as two classifications for nouns. For example, the Spanish word *la jirafa* (the giraffe) is feminine in form. However, it refers to a giraffe in general, regardless of whether it's a male or female giraffe.

Usually, feminine pronouns are used for feminine nouns and masculine pronouns are used for masculine nouns. Therefore, if you know the gender of your noun, you know which pronoun or article to use. For example:
- **a** man: **un** hombre
- **a** woman: **una** mujer
- **the** men: **los** hombres
- **the** women: **las** mujere

Normally, nouns that end in "o" are masculine and those that end in "a" are feminine. NOTE however, that there are several exceptions. Sometimes it's hard to tell whether a noun is masculine or feminine. In these circumstances, you should try looking at a Spanish dictionary. It usually contains gender notations: *f.* for feminine and *m.* for masculine. Anyway, in case you're curious, here are some exceptions to this general rule:

- Words that end in "ista" or those that have and English equivalent ending in "*ist*" can be masculine or feminine. Thus, *dentista* could be either masculine or feminine depending on whether you are referring to a male or a female dentist.
- Shortened versions of certain words retain their original gender. Hence, the word *foto* is feminine since it is a shortened form of *fotografía and la disco is feminine because it's short for la discoteca.*
- *Some words may change in meaning depending on the gender. For example, el papa means "the pope" but la papa means "the potato". Als0, el guardia refers to a policeman or a male guard while la guardia means "vigilance". Here are other examples:*
  - o el aroma — aroma
  - o el Canadá — Canada
  - o el clima — climate
  - o el cólera — cholera (but la cólera, anger)
  - o el cometa — comet (but la cometa, kite)
  - o el cura — priest (but la cura, cure)
  - o el día — day
  - o el agua – water (but the plural is *las aguas*)
  - o al alma – soul (but theplural is *las almas*)
  - o el sofá — sofa
  - o la soprano — female soprano (but el soprano, male soprano)
  - o el tanga — G-string
  - o el telegrama — telegram
  - o el tema — theme, subject

o el teorema — theorem

o el tequila — tequila (short for el licor de Tequila)

o la testigo — female witness (but el testigo, male witness)

There are many exceptions to the "o" masculine and "a" feminine rule. To mention all of them is not within the scope of this book. If however you have doubts, consult your dictionary.

And then a question comes to your mind: what if two or more nouns of mixed genders are described by only one adjective? In this case, the adjective should follow the masculine gender. Example: *El carro y el bicicleta son caros* **(The car and the bicycle are expensive)**

Aside from the common "a" and "o" gender rule, there are other ways to determine the gender of nouns. Some of them are as follows (but remember that there are exceptions):

- Usually, nouns ending in the following suffixes are *feminine* (most of the time): -sión, -ción, -dad, -ía, -za and –itis. Examples are:
  - o la ocasión (occasion)
  - o la nación (nation)
  - o la felicidad (happiness)
  - o la economía (economy)
  - o la verguenza (shame)
  - o la mastitis (mastitis)
- Similarly, nouns with the following endings tend to be *masculine*: -or, -ambre, and –aje.
  - o el calor (heat)
  - o el dolor (pain)
  - o al hambre (hunger)
  - o el mensaje (message)
    - Note: a common exception is *la flor (the flower)*

- Nouns of **Greek origin** ending in "**a**" are usually *masculine* (Note that this is an exception to the general rule of "a" = feminine). Examples are:
  - el problema (problem)
  - el tema (topic/subject)
  - el poema (poem)
- Nouns that end in accented vowels are usually *masculine.* Examples:
  - el rubí (ruby)
  - *el café(the coffee)*
- Infinitives, when used as nouns, are *masculine.* Thus:
  - el cantar (to sing)
  - el trabajar (to work)
  - el viajar (to travel)

- All months and days of the week are *masculine*
- Two-word nouns, which are usually derived from foreign terms, follow the gender of the first noun.
  - el sitio web (website)
- Compound words, formed when verb is followed by a noun, are *masculine.* Example:
  - el dragaminas (minesweeper)
- NUMBERS are *masculine* while LETTERS are *feminine*
  - la b (the letter "b")
  - el 8 (the number "8")
- Names of rivers, oceans and lakes are *masculine*
- Names of mountains are usually *masculine*
  - los Andes
  - los Himalayas
- The names of islands are usually *feminine* because the Spanish word "la isla" is feminine.
  - las Azores (The Azores)

There are other rules with their corresponding exceptions, and newly-adapted words of foreign origin may also change in gender over time, especially if there is a cause for doing so.

As such, whenever you add new words to your dictionary, don't forget to check the gender.

Also, nouns are not the only gender sensitive parts of speech (as I have mentioned earlier). Adjectives and articles can also be either masculine or feminine. We will discuss this in a later chapter.

CHAPTER 6:
CAPITALIZATION

Spanish doesn't capitalize words as much as English. Generally, what is capitalized in Spanish is also capitalized in English but there are many words that English users capitalize and Spanish users do not.

Usually, Spanish speakers only capitalize proper names of people, places, abbreviations for personal titles such as *Sr.* (abbreviation for Señor, Mr. in English) and the first word of literary works such as books, songs, movies and plays.

Personal titles are not capitalized if they are not abbreviated. Example: *¿Conoces a la señora Alvarez?* (Do you know Mrs. Alvarez?) On the other hand, if it were abbreviated, it would look like this: *¿Conoces a la Sra. Alvarez?* And it would still mean the same thing.

These are some classifications of words that are capitalized in English but NOT in Spanish:
- The names of the days of the week, the seasons, and the months of the year
- Names of religions and their adherents and other adjectives derived therefrom
- Nationalities and other adjectives derived from the names of states, countries and cities (although the names of countries and cities themselves are capitalized)
- The names of languages
- The place identifier for specific mountains, lakes, rivers and seas (Example: *el rio Amazona)*
- Ordinal numbers when they are preceded by a name (Example: *Luis catorce "Luis the Fourteenth")*

In summary, you only have to worry about capitalizing nouns under four categories: proper names of **persons**, **places**, **abbreviations** of personal titles and **titles** of literary works. Remember these four key words and you'll be good to go.

CHAPTER 7:
ARTÍCULOS (ARTICLES)

What are articles?

'Articles' is a term used by grammarians to refer to words used to determine whether a noun indicates a specific object within a class, or any object within that type. Used alone, they have little meaning, but together with the noun they modify, you can tell whether the speaker is referring to an object within its class, to the class itself or to something in particular. It is classified into two types: definite and indefinite articles.

Articles are used extensively in Spanish, which is why they should be learned by heart. You only have to be familiar with the rules on how and when to use them and you'll be able to form good Spanish sentences.

Definite Articles (Articulo Definido)

A definite article refers to a word that we use in order to denote that we are referring to something or someone **in particular**. Thus, when we say *"a book"* that means any book will do. But when we say *"the book"*, that means we are referring to a certain book and we usually add a description to indicate which one we are referring to.

As you may already know, the word *"the"* is the only definite article in English. But since nouns, adjectives, articles (and just about everything in Spanish) have numbers and genders; *"the"* has four Spanish equivalents.

They are:

Masculine	*el*	*los*
Feminine	*la*	*las*
	Singular	Plural

In order to achieve good Spanish grammar, nouns and their corresponding modifiers (articles, adjectives) have to agree in **number** and in **gender**.

The definite articles listed above are used whenever the article *"the"* would be used in English. BUT, aside from that there are also other instances where the Spanish use the definite articles which would otherwise be absent in English:

- **When referring to abstract nouns.** In English, when we are talking about intangible nouns or concepts, we do not use articles. But in Spanish, it is common practice. An example would be:
  - *Creo el **la** justicia. (I believe in justice)*
- **With verbs used as the subject of a sentence**. In Spanish, verbs, those in the basic from in particular, can be used as nouns. In such cases, the definite article is used before the verb.
  - *El escribir es difícil. (Writing is difficult.)*
- **Whenever nouns in a series are joined by the conjunction** *"and"*. In English, there is no need to do so, especially when the two nouns are antecedents to only one verb. But in Spanish, it is always required to do so.
  - Example: *Compré **el** traje y **la** corbata (I bought the suit and tie.)*
- **With most of the personal titles of people.**
  - *Voy a la oficina de **la** señora Alfonso (I'm going to the office of Mrs. Alfonso)*
- **When referring to objects or people in a class.**

36

- *Las Españolas quieren hacer dinero (Spanish women want to make money)*
- **Before the days of the week.**
  - *El tren sale **el** domingo. (The train leaves on Sunday)*
- **Before the names of languages.** But there is an exception to this rule. If the name of the language immediately precedes a verb, such as *hablar* (to speak), or if it follows the preposition *"en"*, then no definite article is used. Example:
  - *Hablo bien **el** español (I speak Spanish well)*
  - ***Hablo** español (I speak Spanish)*
  - *No puede escribir **en** español(He can't write in Spanish)*
- **With the names of places**. But this commonly done so only when the place is being modified by an adjective or a prepositional phrase.
  - *Soy de **la** España hermosa. (I come from beautiful Spain)*
  - *Soy de España. (I'm from Spain.)*

In addition, there are also instances wherein the Spanish would add the definite article where the English would not. Such instances are discussed below:

- **When used in a non-restrictive appositive.** An appositive is a word (more often a phrase) which is used to add further description to a noun. A non-restrictive appositive is one that does not limit the meaning of the noun; rather it only adds a description or additional information about it. For example:
  - *Vivo en La Madrid, ciudad hermosa (I live in Madrid, a beautiful city); BUT*
  - *Vivo en Washington, **el** estado (I live in Washinton, the state.)*

Notice that the second sentence uses an indefinite pronoun since the appositive *"el estado"*restricts the meaning of the noun "Washington" to indicate that

you are referring to Washington, the state and not Washington DC.
- **Before ordinal numbers used after the names of people.**
  - ○ *Henry octavo (Henry **the** Eighth)*
- **In some proverbs or maxims and other such statements made to sound in a proverbial manner.**

They are also not used in other statements that do not follow any particular pattern. In this case, you'll just need to become familiar with such phrases.

Indefinite Articles (*Artículo indefinido*)

Indefinite articles are defined as words that make a noun describe anything that is within that class of objects. Meaning, they are used when you are not referring to anything in particular (as opposed to definite pronouns discussed above.).

There are a number of indefinite pronouns in English: *a, an*, and *some*. In Spanish, it has four equivalents:

Masculine	*un*	*Unos*
Feminine	*una*	*Unas*
	Singular	Plural

But take note that the grammatical rules involved in the use of indefinite articles in English and Spanish are not the same. Generally, English uses indefinite articles often, while they have a tendency to be omitted in Spanish. Thus, each time you say *un* or *una* in Spanish, you'll have to add "a" or "an" in English, but the opposite is seldom true.

The addition of indefinite articles to statements where one should not be added is one of the most common mistakes of Spanish learners. However, you can prevent this by becoming familiar with the common instances wherein an indefinite article should NOT be used:

- **In exclamatory statements using the word *"qué"* (what).**
  - *¡Qué coche!* (What **a** car!)
- **Preceding the word "otro" (other).**
  - *Compró otro coche* (He bought **a**nother car.)
- **Before the words "mil" (thousand) and "cien" (hundred)**
  - *Gana mil dólares por mes* (He earns **a** thousand dollars per month)
  - *Tiene cien años.* (She is **a** hundred years old.)
- **Before a noun used after s form of the verb *ser* ("to be"), provided that the noun is unmodified. If the noun is modified (by an adjective, for example) then an article is required.**
  - *Soy dentista.* (I am **a** dentist.); BUT
  - *El es **un** buen dentist.* (He is **a** good dentist.)

  Note that because of the presence of the modifier *"buen"* (good), an indefinite article *"un"* is used.
- **After *con* ("with") and *sin* ("without").**
  - *Come con cuchara pero sin tenedor* (She eats with **a** spoon but without **a** fork.)
- **After forms of the verb *tener* ("to have") and other similar verbs referring to things that people would have or use on at a time.**
  - *No tengo casa* (I don't have **a** house.)

In addition to these rules regarding the omission of indefinite articles, always bear in mind that **the first rule** regarding the use of definite articles (*see **Articulo Definido***) also applies to indefinite articles. That is, two nouns joined by the conjunction "and" require the use of an article.

Otherwise, there would be a change in meaning. Take for example the following sentences:

- **Conozco a un professor y un dentista.** (I know a teacher and a dentist.)
- **Conozco a un professor y dentista.** (I know a teacher who is also a dentist.)

CHAPTER 8:
PRONOMBRES (PRONOUNS)

Ponouns are an important part of speech. They make our conversations easier by allowing us to replace nouns with their corresponding substitutes. Without them, our sentences would be lengthy, redundant, awkward and monotonous.

Take for example the following statements:

Jaime is a good friend. Jaime likes to smile and greet people. Jaime is also smart and Jaime always submits Jaime's homework on time. Jaime is very sensitive about deadlines.

This tedious repetition of Jaime and Jaime's could be easily resolved by the use of pronouns, which would make our sentences smoother and easier to comprehend:

Jaime is a good friend. He likes to smile and greet people. He is also smart and he always submits his homework on time. He is very sensitive about deadlines.

This is true for both English and Spanish. Pronouns replace nouns in a sentence and changes from one form to another depending on how it is used.

Perhaps the only difference between pronouns in English and in Spanish is that almost all Spanish pronouns have gender.

In the next subsections, we shall discuss about the different types of Spanish pronouns and their uses.

Pronombres Sujetos (Subject Pronouns)

Subject pronouns, as the name implies, refers to those that are used to replace the subject of a sentence. Meaning, they refer to the person or thing which performs the action conveyed in the sentence.

There is a need to understand subject pronouns before you learn about Spanish verbs and how to conjugate them. This is because subject pronouns are the basis for choosing the correct form of verb to be used in a sentence.

It is important to note however that once you learn how to conjugate verbs properly, you are free to drop the subject pronoun.

This is because the form of the verb already makes the subject evident. We will discuss about dropping subject pronouns further once we get to proper **verb conjugation**.

The table below contains all the subject pronouns used in Spanish.

Pronombres de Sujeto (Subject Pronouns)

1st person	Singular		Plural	
	yo	I	nosotros/as	we
2nd person	usted (formal)	you	ustedes (formal)	you
	tu (informal)	you	vosotros/as (inf.)	you
3rd person	el	he, it	ellos	they
	ella	she, it	ellas	they

Notice how the English pronoun "you" has four equivalents in Spanish: *usted, ustedes, tu,* and *vosotros.*

The main difference is that the pronoun *"usted"* in all of its forms is equivalent to the **formal** "you" while the other, *"tu"*, is known as the **informal** or **familiar** "you".

There is a need to find out and distinguish which form of "you" should be used, depending on the individual you are speaking to. Using the informal "you" where the formal should be used could make you sound rather disrespectful.

The general rule is that *"tu"* should be used when you are talking to friends, family members, close acquaintances or younger individuals. In other words, it denotes a degree of intimacy between you and the person you are speaking with.

"Usted", on the other hand, is used to refer to persons in authority, older people or to those you do not know or you've just met. It denotes a certain degree of respect and formality.

Whenever you feel confused about which form to use, remember that *"usted"* is safer. *"Tu"* should only be used when talking to a person who is very close to you, or when someone starts addressing you in the same manner (except if they are persons in authority). Indeed, the Spanish even have a verb *"tutear"* which means "to address someone using the pronoun *tu"*.

Note also that in other reading materials in Spanish, *"usted"* is often abbreviated as *"Ud."* (or *Uds.* for plural).

In the case of *feminine plural* pronouns, they are only used when all of the people you are referring to are female. If one of them is male, then you should use the masculine form.

Finally, subject pronouns in Spanish can also be used as *objects of the preposition*. So while you would never say "to he" or "to she" in English, it is perfectly acceptable to say *a el* or *de ella* in Spanish.

There is a need to find out and distinguish which form of "you" should be used, depending on the individual you are speaking to. Using the informal "you" where the formal should be used could make you sound rather disrespectful.

The general rule is that *"tu"* should be used when you are talking to friends, family members, close acquaintances or younger individuals. In other words, it denotes a degree of intimacy between you and the person you are speaking with.

"Usted", on the other hand, is used to refer to persons in authority, older people or to those you do not know or you've just met. It denotes a certain degree of respect and formality.

Whenever you feel confused about which form to use, remember that *"usted"* is safer. *"Tu"* should only be used when talking to a person who is very close to you, or when someone starts addressing you in the same manner (except if they are persons in authority). Indeed, the Spanish even have a verb *"tutear"* which means "to address someone using the pronoun **tu**".

Note also that in other reading materials in Spanish, *"usted"* is often abbreviated as *"Ud."* (or *Uds.* for plural).

In the case of **feminine plural** pronouns, they are only used when all of the people you are referring to are female. If one of them is male, then you should use the **masculine** form.

Finally, subject pronouns in Spanish can also be used as *objects of the preposition*. So while you would never say "to he" or "to she" in English, it is perfectly acceptable to say *a el* or *de ella* in Spanish.

Pronombres Demonstrativos
(Subject Pronouns)

A demonstrative pronoun is one that indicates which object or person is being referred to. There are four demonstrative pronouns in English: *this, that, these* and *those.*

Their equivalents in Spanish are:

	Masculine	Feminine	Neuter
Singular	*éste (this)*	*ésta* (this)	esto
	ése (that)	*ésa* (that)	eso
	aquél (that)	*aquélla* (that)	aquello
Plural	*éstos* (these)	*éstas* (these)	
	ésos (those)	*ésas* (those)	
	aquéllos (those)	*aquéllas* (those)	

Notice how some pronouns have accents. These do not affect their pronunciation.

However, these are used only to distinguish between demonstrative pronouns and demonstrative adjectives. Moreover, unlike the gender rules in other parts of speech, demonstrative pronouns in the masculine gender do not end in "o".

Also, Spanish demonstrative pronouns are complete substitutes for nouns.

Thus, *"this one"* in English is simply translated as *"este"*, *"esta" or "esto"* depending on the gender of the noun that is being replaced. Meaning, there is no need to translate the two words separately.

And you may be wondering, what's the difference between ése and aquél? While both of these are translated as "that" in

English, aquél and its other forms are used for objects that are farther away from the speaker. For example:
- *Me gustan ésas flores.* (I like those flowers.)
- *Me gustan aquéllas flores.* (I like those flowers over there.)

As for the neuter pronouns, they are only used when referring to an event, concept or idea which is not specifically named or mentioned in the same sentence. Example:
- *Tengo que salir a las diez en punto. No olvida **eso**.*
- (I have to leave at 10 o'clock sharp. Don't forget **that**.)

Pronombres Posesivos (Possesive Pronouns)

Possessive pronouns are used to express ownership of an object or close relations with a person.

There are six of them in English: *mine, yours, his, hers, its, ours* and *theirs.* In Spanish, there are only five. But since they change in form according to number and gender, we have twenty in total. They are:

	Masculine		Feminine	
Singular	*mío*	mine	*mía*	mine
	tuyo	yours	*tuya*	yours
	suyo	his, its, theirs	*suya*	hers, its, theirs
	nuestro	ours	*nuestra*	ours
	vuestro	yours	*vuestra*	yours
Plural	*míos*	mine	*mías*	mine
	tuyos	yours	*tuyas*	yours
	suyos	his, its, theirs	*suyas*	hers, its, theirs
	nuestros	ours	*nuestras*	ours
	vuestros	yours	*vuestras*	yours

46

Example: ¿Dónde están **tuyos**? Los **míos** están aquí.
Where are yours? Mine are here. Notice the presence of the article "los" in the second statement.

These are one of the principal differences between the use of possessive pronouns in English and Spanish, since you'd never ever say *"the mine"*.

The exception to this rule is when the possessive pronoun follows any form of the verb *ser*, like *es* or *son* (verbs will be discussed in the next chapter).

Also, the possessive pronoun *suyo* in all of its forms could be quite ambiguous. This is because it can mean either one of the following *his, hers, its* and *theirs.*

Thus, there is a need to rely on context in order to make the statement clear. If however the context doesn't make it clear, it is better to use *de él* or *de ellos.*

*No es mi coche. Es **de ella**.* (It's not my car. It's **hers**.)

Los Pronombres Reflexivos
(Reflexive Pronouns)

Reflexive pronouns are used when the subject of the sentence is also the object of the verb. Meaning, it (the subject) is both the doer and the receiver of the action.

The following are the reflexive pronouns used in Spanish:
- *me* — myself
  - Me veo. (I see myself.)
- *te* — yourself (informal) —
  - ¿Puedes verte? (Can you see yourself?)
- *se* — himself, herself, itself, themselves, yourself (formal), yourselves (formal), each other
  - La historia se repite. (History repeats itself.)

- o El gato se ve en el espejo. (The cat sees himself in the mirror.)
- **nos** — ourselves, each other
  - o Nos respetamos. (We respect ourselves, or we respect each other.)
  - o No podemos vernos. (We can't see each other, or we can't see ourselves.)
- **os** — yourselves (informal), each other
  - o Es evidente que os queréis. (It's obvious that you love each other, or it's obvious you love yourselves.)
  - o Podéis ayudaros. (You can help yourselves, or you can help each other.)

Notice the ambiguity in meaning when using reflexive pronouns in the second person formal as well the third person. You'll have to rely on context to understand what the speaker intends to say.

At times, additional phrases are added after the verb to clarify the meaning or to give emphasis. Thus, the sentence *Nos respetamos* could be rephrased as *Nos respetamos a sí mismos (We respect ourselves.)* or *Nos respetamos el uno a otro (We respect each other.)*

Pronombres Indefinidos

Indefinite pronouns, like an indefinite article (discussed earlier), are used when you are **not** referring to any particular person or object. The only difference between them is that indefinite pronouns replace nouns instead of simply modifying them. Here is a list of the known Spanish indefinite pronouns:
- *algo* — something
  - o *¿Aprendiste algo esta mañana?*
  - o (Did you learn**something** this mmorning?)
- *alguien* — someone, somebody, anyone, anybody

- o *Necesito a **alguien** que pueda hablar español.*
  - o (I need **someone** who can speak Spanish.)
- ***alguno, alguna, algunos, algunas*** — one, some (things or people)
  - o *¿Quieres **alguno** más?* (Do you want **one/some** more?)
- ***Cualquiera*** — anybody, anyone
  - o ***Cualquiera** puede tocar la guitarra.*
    (**Anyone** can play the guitar.)
- ***Mucho/a, muchos/as*** — much, many
  - o *La escuela tiene **mucho** que ofrecer.*
    (The school has **much** to offer.)
- ***nada*** — nothing
  - o ***Nada** me parece cierto.* (***Nothing*** seems certain to me.)
  - o ***No** tengo **nada**.* (I have ***nothing***.)

Note that when *nada*is preceded by a verb, the part of the word before theverb is also put in negative form, making a double negative, which is unacceptable in English.

- ***nadie*** — nobody, no one
  - o ***No** conozco a **nadie**.* (I know ***nobody***.)

Here the double negative appears again, the same case with the pronoun *nada*.

- ***ninguno, ninguna*** — none, nobody, no one
  - o ***Ninguna** de ellos va al parque.* (None of them are going to the park.)
  - o ***No** conozco a **ninguno**.* (I know nobody.)

The pronoun *ninguno* in the second sentence also follows a double-negative form if it is found after the verb and may be used interchangeably with *nadie*

- *otro, otra, otros, otras* — another, other one, another one, other ones, others
  - Los *otros* van al parque. (The **others** are going to the park.)

Note that "another one" in Spanish is not translated as "un/una otro". It is one of the instances where the indefinite article is omitted (see ***Articulo Indefinido***). Rather, *otros* and other related pronouns can be combined with a definite article (el, la, los or las) as in the second example.

- *Poco/a, pocos/as* — little, little bit, few, a few
  - *Pocos* van al parque. (**A few** are going to the park.)
- *todo, todos/as* — everything, all, everyone
  - *Todos* van al parque. (**All** are going to the park.)
- *Uno/a, unos/as* — one, some
  - *Unos* quieren ganar más. (Some want to earn more.)

Pronombre Relativo (Relative Pronoun)

Relative pronouns are those used to introduce a statement that adds additional information or description about a noun.

In the phrase *"the girl who is dancing"* for example, "who" serves as our relative pronoun. "Who is dancing" gives us further information about which girl we are talking about, or what the girl is doing.

The most common relative pronoun in use in Spanish is **que**. It is equivalent to the English *"who, which or that"*.

Mi madre es la mujer que salió. **(My mother is the lady who left.)**

Los libros que son importantes en nuestra vida son aquellos que nos enseñan a superarnos.

(The books **that** are important in our lives are those **which** teach us to improve ourselves.)

Other relative pronouns are:
- **quien, quienes** — who, whom
  - Es el dentista de **quien** le dije.
    He is the dentist whom I told you about.
- **El/la/lo cual, los/las cuales**— which, who, whom
  - Maria es la mujer con la **cual** vas a trabajar.
  - Maria is the woman with **whom** you are going to work.
- **El/la/lo que, los que, las que** — which, who, whom
  - Maria es la mujer con **la que** vas a trabajar.
  - Maria is the woman with **whom** you are going to work.

Note that the second and third pronouns are interchangeable when they are taken to mean the same thing.
- **Cuyo/a, cuyos/as** — whose
  - Es la dentista *cuyo* hijo tiene lacasa grande.
  - She is the teacher *whose* son has the big house.

Pronombres Interrogativos
(Interrogative Pronouns)

Spanish interrogative pronouns, as the name implies, are used when asking a question. Like their English counterparts, they are mostly written at the very beginning, or very near the beginning, of every sentence.

The following are some of the most common Spanish interrogative pronouns. Remember that it must agree with the number and gender (if applicable) of the noun that it replaces:

- *quién, quiénes* — who, whom
  - ¿*Quién* es tu amigo? (Who is your friend?)
  - ¿De *quién* es esta billetera? (Whose wallet is this?)
  - ¿Para *quiénes* son los regalos? (Whom are the gifts for?)
- *qué* — what
  - ¿*Qué* es esto? (**What** is this?)
  - ¿En *qué* piensas? (**What** are you thinking about?)
  - ¿De *qué* hablas? (**What** are you talking about?)

Note however that the phrases *"por qué"* and *"para qué"* are understood to mean *"**why?**"* instead of *"what?"* These two phrases are interchangeable, except that *por qué* is used more often and *para qué* can more specifically be translated as *"what for?"* Examples:
  - ¿*Para qué* estudiaba español?
    Why did you study Spanish? or
    What did you study Spanish for?
  - ¿*Por qué* se rompió el coche?
    Why did the car break down?
- *dónde* — where
  - ¿*Dónde* está? (**Where** is it?)

Note that the phrase *"de dónde"* means *"**where from?**"* and *"Adónde"* means *"to **where?**"*
  - ¿*De dónde* es Alberto? (**Where** is Alberto **from**?)
  - ¿*Adónde* vas? (**Where** are you going **to**?)
- *cuándo* — when
  - ¿*Cuándo* salimos? (***When*** are we leaving?)

The phrase *"hasta cuándo?"* means, "**until when?**"
  - ¿*Hasta cuándo* quedan ustedes? (Until when are you staying?)
- cuál, cuáles — which one, which ones
  - ¿*Cuál* prefieres? (Which one do you prefer?)

Cuál and *cuáles* are usually used when you are referring to one out of several possible choices.

- **cómo** — how
  - ○ **¿Cómo** estás? (**How** are you?)
- **Cuánto/a, cuántos/as** — how much, how many
  - ○ **¿Cuánto** hay? (How much is there?)
  - ○ **¿Cuántos**? (How many?)

The accent marks present in the vowels of these pronouns do not affect the pronunciation. However, they are only used to set them apart from words of similar forms or spellings that function differently.

Thus, if any of these words are used in a statement rather than a question (which is possible but is beyond the scope of this book), the accent marks would be removed.

You may also notice that Spanish is unique in terms of punctuating interrogative statements. It used an inverted punctuation before the sentence. This is also tru for the case of an exclamation/interjection (!).

The pattern for asking questions is Spanish is similar to that in English. The interrogative pronoun is usually followed by the verb.

Pronombres Objeto Verbales
(Verbal Object Pronouns)

Pronouns used as objects of the verb are of two types: **direct** and **indirect object**. But before we discuss these variations, here is a list of the verbal object pronouns in Spanish:

Direct Object			Indirect object	
me	me	Ella me ama (she loves me).	me	Ella me dio el anillo (She gave me the ring).
te	you	Ella te ama.	te	Ella te dio el anillo.
lo	him, it	Ella lo/la ama.	le	Ella le dio el anillo.
la	her, it	Ella lo/la ama.	nos	Ella nos dio el anillo.
nos	us	Ella nos ama.	os	Ella os dio el anillo.
os	you	Ella os ama.	les	Ella les dio el anillo.
los	them, you	Ella los/las ama.		
las	them, you	Ella los/las ama.		

Sometimes people find it difficult to point out the direct and indirect objects or distinguish one form the other. The simplest explanation is that the **direct object** is the thing being *acted upon* by the verb while the **indirect object** refers to the thing or person for *whom* it is done. Thus, when one says "I gave her a ring.", "ring" is the direct object since it tells us WHAT it being given and "her" is the indirect object since it tells us to WHOM the ring was given.

The difference between the Spanish and English way of constructing these types of sentences is that in Spanish, the object goes before the verb. Thus, "She sees me" is translated as "Ella me ve" instead of "Ella ve me".

Pronombre Preposicional
(Prepositional Pronouns)

As may have already guessed, these are pronouns that are found next to the prepositions in a sentence. And just in case you think a definition is being called for, prepositions refer to those words which define the *relationship* between the verb and the other words in a sentence. A few examples will make this clear. But first, here's a list of the prepositional pronouns. Notice that some of them are very similar to subject pronouns except for the first and second person singular. Such is Spanish. Some of its words overlap and have multiple functions, so you'll have to rely on context to understand what a person is trying to say.

- *mí* – me
  - El anillo es para mí. The ring is for me.

In this sentence *"para"* (translated *for*) is our preposition and *"mí"* (*me)* is the prepositional pronoun. The preposition tells is the relationship between the verb and the prepositional pronoun.

- *ti* (informal second-person singular, equivalent of "you")
  - El anillo es para ti. The ring is for you.
- *usted* (formal second-person singular, equivalent of "you")
  - El anillo es para usted. The ring is for you.
- *él* (third-person masculine singular, equivalent of "him" or "it")
  - El anillo es para él. The ring is for him. Miro debajo él. I am looking under it.
- *ella* (third-person feminine singular, equivalent of "her" or "it")
  - El anillo es para ella. The ring is for her. Miro debajo él. I am looking under it.
- *Nosotros/as* (first-person plural, equivalent of "us")

o   El anillo es para nosotros. The ring is for us.
- *Vosotros/as* (second-person informal plural, equivalent of "you")
  o   El anillo es para vosotros. The ring is for you.
- *ustedes* (second-person formal plural, equivalent of "you")
  o   El anillo es para ustedes. The ring is for you.
- *Ellos/as* (third-person plural, equivalent of "them")
  o   El anillo es para ellos. The ring is for them.

Pronombre Objeto Preposicional (Prepositional Object Pronouns)

The phrase "I'm going to..." doesn't make any sense, does it? You can tell that there's something missing. In Spanish, just as in English, you'll need an object to your preposition in order to express a complete idea. These objects are often in theform of **nouns** and **pronouns** (or other parts of speech that function as such). Some examples will make this clear:

- *mí* — me
  o   Salieron sin *mí*. They left without **me**.
- *ti* — you (singular informal)
  o   Hablan de **ti**. They are talking about **you**.

Note that when these first two pronouns are used with *"con"*(translated as "with), instead of **con mí** and **con ti**, they take the form of *"conmigo"* and *"contigo"*

  o   **Voy *contigo*.** I'm coming **with you**.
- *usted* — you (singular formal)
  o   Las flores son para *usted*. The flowers are for **you**.
- *él, ella* — him, her
  o   Fue escrito por *ella*. It was written by **her**.
- *Nosotros/as* — us
  o   Vienen tras *nosotros*. They are coming after **us**.
- *vosotros, vosotras* — you (plural informal)
  o   Salgo sin *vosotros*. I am leaving without **you**.

- *Ellos/as* — them
  - o La comida no es para *ellos*. The food isn't for **them**.

Preposicionales Pronombres Reflexivos (Prepositional Reflexive pronouns)

These are used when the object of a preposition refers back to the subject of a sentence. There are equivalent to the words *myself, yourself, himself, herself, itself, yourselves* and *themselves* in English. For example, in the statement *(Yo) Compré comida para mí (I bought food for myself)*, the prepositional reflexive pronoun is *mí* (myself), *para* (for) is the preposition and the implied subject is *yo* (I). Here's another list for reference:

- *mí* — myself
  - o Lo compré para mí. (I bought it for myself.)
- *ti* — yourself (informal)
  - o Lo compraste para ti. (You bought it for yourself.)
- *sí* — himself, herself, itself, themselves, yourself (formal), yourselves (formal)
  - o Alfredo lo compró para sí. (Alfredo bought it for **himself**.)
  - o Ustedes lo compraron para sí. (You bought it for **yourselves**.)

Sí here should not be mistaken for *sí (meaning "yes")* or the unstressed *si* meaning "if". Such similarities are common in Spanish (as you may have already noticed with all these lists of similarly-spelled pronouns). Again, context is important.

Also, like the forms **conmigo** and **contigo**, this pronoun when used with *con* also takes a similar form: *consigo*.

- *nosotros* — ourselves
  - o Lo compramos para *nosotros*. (We bought it for **ourselves**.)

- *vosotros* — yourselves (informal)
  - o Lo comprasteis para **vosotros**. (You bought it for **<u>yourselves</u>**.)

That just about wraps it up for our lesson on pronouns.Don't forget that although this is standard Spanish, there could be regional variations since language is dynamic.

The second person informal (*ti*) is usually only widely used in Spain.

CHAPTER 9:
EL VERBOS (VERBS)

The verb is the most essential part of a sentence. It's the part that tells an action and describes what happens or describes the state of being of the subject. Thus, you can't have a sentence without one. In fact, a verb can becoe a sentence in itself and is the minimum requirement for conveying a complete thought. Verbs, whether in Spanish or English, have to be conjugated properly in order to convey the correct meaning.

Conjugating verbs tells us **who** performed the action, **when** the action is performed and **how** the verb s related to the other words in the sentence. The verbs in Spanish are extensively conjugated, each one agreeing with the subject of the sentence in both number and gender. This is the reason why the subject of the sentence is sometimes dropped or implied since *the form of the verb in itself will make the subject obvious.*

The most basic form of the Spanish verb is the **infinitive**.

Its English equivalents are composed of the preposition "to" plus the base form of the verb. *"to dance", "to sing" and "to write"* are a few examples.There are three types of verbs in Spanish.

They are classified according to their endings: *-ar, er,* and *ir.*

The first one, *-ar,* appears most frequently. The pattern for conjugating verbs depends on these endings. Take note, however, that there are exceptions. Spanish also has its irregular verbs. In this case, you'll have to familiarize each one.

The good news is that most of the verbs in Spanish are regular verbs.

Thus, if you learn the pattern on conjugating these verbs, you'll automatically know how to conjugate a thousand others.

Note also that there are some verbs that do not exist in all conjugated forms. These are called *defective verbs (verbos defectivos)*.

Conjugación de los Verbos (Conjugating Verbs)

To learn about how to conjugate Spanish verbs, you'll have to be familiar with the different verb tenses used in Spanish: presente indicative (present), pretérito (past), futuro (future), participio (past participle), and imperativo (imperative).

You may have learned about this in your English grammar class but for the sake of clarity, this is what the tenses/moods denote:
- Present – refers to action that is currently being done or is continually done
- Past –refers to action that the doer has already accomplished
- Future – actions that will be done (or are intended to be done) in the future
- Participle (or past participle) – is a kind of past tense for that uses the introductory "have" before the past participle form of the verb to indicate action which has been done only recently or at a specific point I the past
- Imperative – is the mood of a verb (not a tense) which is used when making commands or requests. But for our intents and purposes, we shall include the

imperative mood in conjugating our verbs in order to make it easier for you to form command sentences. ☺

We shall now deal with conjugating –ar verbs first, followed by the rest of the regular verbs before we deal with the irregular ones.

Below is a table that shows the pattern for conjugating –ar verbs using the word **hablar** (to speak):

PRESENTE INDICATIVO	PRETÉRITO	FUTURO	PARTICIPIO	IMPERATIVO
yo <u>hablo</u>	yo **hablé**	yo **hablaré**	**hablado**	
tú <u>hablas</u>	tú **hablaste**	tú **hablarás**	**hablado**	**habla** (tú), **no hables** (tú)
usted/el/ ella <u>habla</u>	usted/él/ella **habló**	usted/él/ ella **hablará**	**hablado**	**hable** (usted)
nosotros/as hablamos	nosotros/as **hablamos**	nosotros/as **hablaremos**	**hablado**	**hablemos** (nosotros/as)
vosotros/as <u>habláis</u>	vosotros/as **hablasteis**	vosotros/as **hablaréis**	**hablado**	**hablad** (vosotros/as), **no habléis** (vosotros/as)
ustedes/ ellos/ellas <u>hablan</u>	ustedes/ellos/ellas **hablaron**	ustedes/ellos/ellas **hablarán**	**hablado**	**hablen** (ustedes)

Examples:
- Yo hablo español. I speak Spanish.
- ¿Hablas tú español? Do you speak Spanish?
- And this is the part where you say,

61

- *"Sí, hablo (un poco de)*español."*
- Yes, I speak (a little) Spanish. ☺

For –*er* verbs, we use beber (to drink):

PRESENTE INDICATIVO	PRETÉRITO	FUTURO	PARTICIPIO	IMPERATIVO
yo bebo	yo bebí	yo beberé	bebido	
tú bebes	tú bebiste	tú beberás	bebido	bebe (tú), no bebas (tú)
usted/él/ella bebe	usted/él/ella bebió	usted/él/ella beberá	bebido	beba (usted)
nosotros/as bebemos	nosotros/as bebimos	nosotros/as beberemos	bebido	bebamos (nosotros/as)
vosotros/as bebéis	vosotros/as bebisteis	vosotros/as beberéis	bebido	bebed (vosotros/as) no bebáis (vosotros/as)
ustedes/ ellos/ellas beben	ustedes/ellos/ellas bebieron	ustedes/ ellos/ellas beberán	bebido	beban (ustedes)

For –*ir* verbs, the more popular example is vivir (to live):

PRESENTE INDICATIVO	PRETÉRITO	FUTURO	PARTICIPIO	IMPERATIVO
yo vivo	yo viví	yo viviré	vivido	
tú vives	tú viviste	tú vivirás	vivido	vive (tú), no vivas (tú)
usted/él/ ella vive	usted/él/ella vivió	usted/él/ ella vivirá	vivido	viva (usted)
nosotros/as vivimos	nosotros/as vivimos	nosotros/as viviremos	vivido	vivamos (nosotros/as)
vosotros/as vivís	vosotros/as vivisteis	vosotros/as viviréis	vivido	vivid (vosotros/as), no viváis (vosotros/as)
ustedes/ ellos/ellas viven	ustedes/ellos/ellas vivieron	ustedes/ ellos/ellas vivirán	vivido	vivan (ustedes)

62

Take special note of the endings for each conjugated form. The pattern is the same for all regular verbs. And because we can't take a similar approach when dealing with the irregular ones, we're just going to have to conjugate some of the most common irregular verbs one by one. It's not possible to tackle all of them within this single work but take time to familiarize their respective patterns. Once you master these verbs, you will have command of a host of other *verbos españoles.*

Abrir "to open" *(including cubrir "to cover" and discubrir "to find out")*

Present indicative	**yo abro, tú abres, usted/él/ella abre, nosotros/as abrimos, vosotros/as abrís, ustedes/ellos/ellas abren**
Preterite (pretérito)	yo abrí, tu abriste, usted/él/ella abrió, nosotros/as abrimos, vosotros/as abristeis, ustedes/ellos/ellas abrieron
Future (futuro)	yo abriré, tú abrirás, usted/él/ella abrirá, nosotros/as abriremos, vosotros/as abriréis, ustedes/ellos/ellas abrirán
Imperative (imperativo)	abre (tú), no abras (tú), abra (usted), abramos (nosotros/as), abrid (vosotros/as), no abráis (vosotros/as), abran (ustedes)

Andar "to walk"

Present indicative (presente del indicativo)	**yo ando, tú andas, usted/él/ella anda, nosotros/as andamos, vosotros/as andáis, ustedes/ellos/ellas andan**
Preterite (pretérito)	yo **anduve**, tu **anduviste**, usted/él/ella **anduvo**, nosotros/as **anduvimos**, vosotros/as **anduvisteis**, ustedes/ellos/ellas **anduvieron**
Future (futuro)	yo andaré, tú andarás, usted/él/ella andará, nosotros/as andaremos, vosotros/as andaréis, ustedes/ellos/ellas andarán
Imperative (imperativo)	anda (tú), no andes (tú), ande (usted), andemos (nosotros/as), andad (vosotros/as), no andéis (vosotros/as), anden (ustedes)

Buscar "to search for" *(and other verbs ending in –car)*

Present indicative	**yo busco, tú buscas, usted/él/ella busca, nosotros/as buscamos, vosotros/as buscáis, ustedes/ellos/ellas buscan**
Preterite (pretérito)	**yo busqué**, tu buscaste, usted/él/ella buscó, nosotros/as buscamos, vosotros/as buscasteis, ustedes/ellos/ellas buscaron
Future (futuro)	yo buscaré, tú buscarás, usted/él/ella buscará, nosotros/as buscaremos, vosotros/as buscaréis, ustedes/ellos/ellas buscarán
Imperative (imperativo)	busca (tú), no **busques** (tú), **busque** (usted), **busquemos** (nosotros/as), buscad (vosotros/as), no **busquéis** (vosotros/as), **busquen** (ustedes)

Conocer "to know" (including agradecer "to thank", complacer "to please", crecer "to grow", desconocer "to ignore", desobedecer "to disobey", florecer "to flourish", merecer "to earn", nacer "to be born", obedecer "to obey", ofrecer "to offer", perecer "to perish", pertenecer "to belong", and reconocer "to recognize")

Present indicative	**yo** conozco, **tú conoces, usted/él/ella conoce, nosotros/as conocemos, vosotros/as conocéis, ustedes/ellos/ellas conocen**
Preterite (pretérito)	yo conocí, tu conociste, usted/él/ella conoció, nosotros/as conocimos, vosotros/as conocisteis, ustedes/ellos/ellas conocieron
Future (futuro)	yo conoceré, tú conocerás, usted/él/ella conocerá, nosotros/as conoceremos, vosotros/as conoceréis, ustedes/ellos/ellas conocerán
Imperative (imperativo)	co oce (tú), no **conozcas** (tú), **conozca** (usted), **conozcamos** (nosotros/as), conoced (vosotros/as), no **conozcáis** (vosotros/as), conozcan (ustedes)

Contar "to count" (and other -ar stem-changing verbs)

Present indicative	**yo cuento, tú cuentas, usted/él/ella cuenta, nosotros/as contamos, vosotros/as contáis, ustedes/ellos/ellas cuentan**
Preterite (pretérito)	yo conté, tu contaste, usted/él/ella contó, nosotros/as contamos, vosotros/as contasteis, ustedes/ellos/ellas contaron
Future (futuro)	yo contaré, tú contarás, usted/él/ella contará, nosotros/as contaremos, vosotros/as contaréis, ustedes/ellos/ellas contarán
Imperative (imperativo)	**cuenta** (tú), no **cuentes** (tú), **cuente** (usted), contemos (nosotros/as), contad (vosotros/as), no contéis (vosotros/as), **cuenten** (ustedes)

Dar "to give"

Present indicative	**yo doy (I give), tú das (you give), usted/él/ella da (you give / he/she gives), nosotros/as damos (we give), vosotros/as daís (you give), ustedes/ellos/ellas dan (you/they give)**
Preterite (pretérito)	yo di (I gave), tu diste (you gave), usted/él/ella dio (you/he/she gave), nosotros/as dimos (we gave), vosotros/as disteis (you gave), ustedes/ellos/ellas dieron (you/they gave)
Future (futuro)	yo daré (I will give), tú darás (you will give), usted/él/ella dará (you/she/she will give), nosotros/as daremos (we will give), vosotros/as daréis (you will give), ustedes/ellos/ellas darán (you/they will give)
Imperative (imperativo)	da tú (give), no des tú (don't give), dé usted (give), demos nosotros/as (let's give), dad vosotros/as (give), no deis vosotros/as (don't give), den ustedes (give)

Decir "to say" (includingcondecir "to agree", contradecir "to contradict", desdecir "to belie" and predecir "to predict")

Present indicative	**yo digo, tú dices, usted/él/ella dice, nosotros/as decimos, vosotros/as decís, ustedes/ellos/ellas dicen**
Preterite (pretérito)	yo dije, tu dijiste, usted/él/ella dijo, nosotros/as dijimos, vosotros/as dijisteis, ustedes/ellos/ellas dijeron
Future (futuro)	yo diré, tú dirás, usted/él/ella dirá, nosotros/as diremos, vosotros/as diréis, ustedes/ellos/ellas dirán
Imperative (imperativo)	di tú, no digas tú, diga usted, digamos nosotros/as, decid vosotros/as, no digáis vosotros/as, digan ustedes

Entender"to understand" (and other -er stem-changing verbs, including: ascender "to ascend", attender "to serve", defender "to defend", descender "to go down", and perder "to lose")

Present indicative	**yo entiendo, tú entiendes, usted/él/ella entiende, nosotros/as entendemos, vosotros/as entendéis, ustedes/ellos/ellas entienden**
Preterite (pretérito)	yo entendí, tu entendiste, usted/él/ella entendió, nosotros/as entendimos, vosotros/as entendisteis, ustedes/ellos/ellas entendieron
Future (futuro)	yo entenderé, tú entenderás, usted/él/ella entenderá, nosotros/as entenderemos, vosotros/as entenderéis, ustedes/ellos/ellas entenderán
Imperative (imperativo)	entiende (tú), no entiendas (tú), entienda usted, entendamos (nosotros/as), entended (vosotros/as), no entendáis (vosotros/as), entiendan ustedes

Estar "to be"

Present indicative	**yo estoy, tú estás, usted/él/ella está, nosotros/as estamos, vosotros/as estáis, ustedes/ellos/ellas están**
Preterite (pretérito)	yo estuve, tu estuviste, usted/él/ella estuvo, nosotros/as estuvimos, vosotros/as estuvisteis, ustedes/ellos/ellas estuvieron
Future (futuro)	yo estaré, tú estarás, usted/él/ella estará, nosotros/as estaremos, vosotros/as estaréis, ustedes/ellos/ellas estarán
Imperative (imperativo)	está (tú), no estés (tú), esté (usted), estemos (nosotros/as), estad (vosotros/as), no estéis (vosotros/as), estén (ustedes)

Gozar "to enjoy" (and other verbs ending in –zar, such as: abrazar "to hug", adelgazar "to slim down", amenazar "to threaten", aplazar "to postpone", aterrizar "to move", avanzar "to land", bostezar "to yawn", cazar "to chase", cristalizar "to crystallize", cruzar "to cross", descalzar "to remove", deslizar "to slide", destrozar "to destroy", disfrazar "to disguise", economizer "to save", embarazar "to be pregnant", encabezar "to lead", endulzar "to sweeten", garantizar "to ensure", izar "to lift", lanzar "to throw", organizer "to arrange", realizer "to perform", rezar "to pray", rechazar "to reject", trazar "to draw" and utilizar "to use")

Present indicative	yo gozo, tú gozas, usted/él/ella goza, nosotros/as gozamos, vosotros/as gozáis, ustedes/ellos/ellas gozan
Preterite (pretérito)	yo gocé, tu gozaste, usted/él/ella gozó, nosotros/as gozamos, vosotros/as gozasteis, ustedes/ellos/ellas gozaron
Future (futuro)	yo gozaré, tú gozarás, usted/él/ella gozará, nosotros/as gozaremos, vosotros/as gozaréis, ustedes/ellos/ellas gozarán
Imperative (imperativo)	goza (tú), no goces (tú), goce (usted), gocemos (nosotros/as), gozad (vosotros/as), no gocéis (vosotros/as), gocen (ustedes)

Haber "to possess"

Present indicative	yo he, tú has, usted/él/ella ha (hay), nosotros/as hemos, vosotros/as habéis, ustedes/ellos/ellas han (hay)
Preterite (pretérito)	yo hube , tú hubiste , usted/él/ella hubo , nosotros/as hubimos, vosotros/as hubisteis , ustedes/ellos/ellas hubieron
Future (futuro)	yo habré, tú habrás, usted/él/ella habrá, nosotros/as habremos, vosotros/as habréis, ustedes/ellos/ellas habrán
Imperative (imperativo)	*El verbo haber is never used in the imperative mood*

Ir "to go"

Present indicative	**yo voy, tú vas, usted/él/ella va, nosotros/as vamos, vosotros/as vais, ustedes/ellos/ellas van**
Preterite (pretérito)	yo fui, tu fuiste, usted/él/ella fue, nosotros/as fuimos, vosotros/as fuisteis, ustedes/ellos/ellas fueron
Future (futuro)	yo iré, tú irás, usted/él/ella irá, nosotros/as iremos, vosotros/as iréis, ustedes/ellos/ellas irán
Imperative (imperativo)	ve (tú), no vayas (tú), vaya (usted), vamos or vayamos (nosotros/as), id (vosotros/as), no vayáis (vosotros/as), vayan (ustedes)

Pagar "to pay" (and other verbs ending in –gar, namely: apagar "to turn off", cargar "to load", despegar "to launch", entregar "to deliver", juzgar "to assess", llegar "to reach", obligar "to bind", pegar "to stick", tragar "to swallow", and vengar "to avenge")

Present indicative	**yo pago, tú pagas, usted/él/ella paga, nosotros/as pagamos, vosotros/as pagáis, ustedes/ellos/ellas pagan**
Preterite (pretérito)	yo pagué, tu pagaste, usted/él/ella pagó, nosotros/as pagamos, vosotros/as pagasteis, ustedes/ellos/ellas pagaron
Future (futuro)	yo pagaré, tú pagarás, usted/él/ella pagará, nosotros/as pagaremos, vosotros/as pagaréis, ustedes/ellos/ellas pagarán
Imperative (imperativo)	paga (tú), no pagues (tú), pague (usted), paguemos (nosotros/as), pagad (vosotros/as), no paguéis (vosotros/as), paguen (ustedes)

Pensar "to think" (same pattern goes for: acertar "to hit", alentar "to encourage", apretar "to push", arrendar "to lease", atravesar "to cross", calendar to heat up", cerrar "to close", confesar "to confess", despertar "to awaken", encerrar"to lock", enterrar "to burry", gobernar "to govern", helar "to freeze", manifestar "to show", merendar "to snack", recomendar "to recommend", reventar "to burst", sembrar "to plant", and sentar "to lay")

Present indicative	**yo pienso, tú piensas, usted/él/ella piensa, nosotros/as pensamos, vosotros/as pensáis, ustedes/ellos/ellas piensan**
Preterite (pretérito)	yo pensé, tu pensaste, usted/él/ella pensó, nosotros/as pensamos, vosotros/as pensasteis, ustedes/ellos/ellas pensaron
Future (futuro)	yo pensaré, tú pensarás, usted/él/ella pensará, nosotros/as pensaremos, vosotros/as pensaréis, ustedes/ellos/ellas pensarán
Imperative (imperativo)	piensa tú, no pienses tú, piense usted, pensemos nosotros/as, pensad vosotros/as, no penséis vosotros/as, piensen ustedes

Poder "to be able"

Present indicative	**yo puedo, tú puedes, usted/él/ella puede, nosotros/as podemos, vosotros/as podéis, ustedes/ellos/ellas pueden**
Preterite (pretérito)	yo pude, tu pudiste, usted/él/ella pudo, nosotros/as pudimos, vosotros/as pudisteis, ustedes/ellos/ellas pudieron
Future (futuro)	yo podré, tú podrás, usted/él/ella podrá, nosotros/as podremos, vosotros/as podréis, ustedes/ellos/ellas podrán
Imperative (imperativo)	puede (tú), no puedas (tú), pueda (usted), podamos (nosotros/as), poded (vosotros/as), no podáis (vosotros/as), puedan (ustedes)

Poner "to put" (and other verbs ending in –poner: componer "to compose", disponer "to dispose", exponer "to expose", imponer "to impose", oponer "to oppose", proponer "to propose", reponer "to replace" and suponer "to assume")

Present indicative	yo pongo, tú pones, usted/él/ella pone, nosotros/as ponemos, vosotros/as ponéis, ustedes/ellos/ellas ponen
Preterite (pretérito)	yo puse, tu pusiste, usted/él/ella puso, nosotros/as pusimos, vosotros/as pusisteis, ustedes/ellos/ellas pusieron
Future (futuro)	yo pondré, tú pondrás, usted/él/ella pondrá, nosotros/as pondremos, vosotros/as pondréis, ustedes/ellos/ellas pondrán
Imperative (imperativo)	pon (tú), no pongas (tú), ponga (usted), pongamos (nosotros/as), poned (vosotros/as), no pongáis (vosotros/as), pongan (ustedes)

Querer "to want/to love"

Present indicative	yo quiero, tú quieres, usted/él/ella quiere, nosotros/as queremos, vosotros/as queréis, ustedes/ellos/ellas quieren
Preterite (pretérito)	yo quise, tu quisiste, usted/él/ella quiso, nosotros/as quisimos, vosotros/as quisisteis, ustedes/ellos/ellas quisieron
Future (futuro)	yo querré, tú querrás, usted/él/ella querrá, nosotros/as querremos, vosotros/as querréis, ustedes/ellos/ellas querrán
Imperative (imperativo)	quiere (tú) (want), no quieras (tú) (don't want), quiera (usted) (want), queramos (nosotros/as) (let's want), quered (vosotros/as) (want), no queráis (vosotros/as) (don't want), quieran (ustedes) (want)

Saber "to know"

Present indicative	**yo sé (I know), tú sabes (you know), usted/él/ella sabe (you know, he/she knows), nosotros/as sabemos (we know), vosotros/as sabéis (you know), ustedes/ellos/ellas saben (you/they know)**
Preterite (pretérito)	yo supe (I knew), tú supiste (you knew), usted/él/ella supo (you, he/she knew), nosotros/as supimos (we knew), vosotros/as supisteis (you knew), ustedes/ellos/ellas supieron (they knew)
Future (futuro)	yo sabré (I will know), tú sabrás (you will know), usted/él/ella sabrá (you/he/she will know), nosotros/as sabremos (we will know), vosotros/as sabréis (you will know), ustedes/ellos/ellas sabrán (they will know)
Imperative (imperativo)	sabe tú (know), no sepas tú (don't know), sepa usted (know), sepamos nosotros/as (let us know), sabed vosotro/s (know), no sepáis vosotros/as (don't know), sepan ustedes (know)

Salir "to leave" (including sobresalir meaning, "to stand out")

Present indicative	**yo salgo, tú sales, usted/él/ella sale, nosotros/as salimos, vosotros/as salís, ustedes/ellos/ellas salen**
Preterite (pretérito)	yo salí, tu saliste, usted/él/ella salió, nosotros/as salimos, vosotros/as salisteis, ustedes/ellos/ellas salieron
Future (futuro)	yo saldré, tú saldrás, usted/él/ella saldrá, nosotros/as saldremos, vosotros/as saldréis, ustedes/ellos/ellas saldrán
Imperative (imperativo)	sal (tú), no salgas (tú), salga (usted), salgamos (nosotros/as), salid (vosotros/as), no salgáis (vosotros/as), salgan (ustedes)

Sentir "to feel" (and some other -ir stem-changing verbs)

Present indicative	**yo siento, tú sientes, usted/él/ella siente, nosotros/as sentimos, vosotros/as sentís, ustedes/ellos/ellas sienten**
Preterite (pretérito)	yo sentí, tú sentiste, usted/él/ella sintió, nosotros/as sentimos, vosotros/as sentisteis, ustedes/ellos/ellas sintieron
Future (futuro)	yo sentiré, tú sentirás, usted/él/ella sentirá, nosotros/as sentiremos, vosotros/as sentiréis, ustedes/ellos/ellas sentirán
Imperative (imperativo)	siente (tú), no sientas (tú), sienta (usted), sintamos (nosotros/as), sentid (vosotros/as), no sintáis (vosotros/as), sientan (ustedes)

Ser "is/am" (auxiliary verb)

Present indicative	**yo soy, tú eres, usted/él/ella es, nosotros/as somos, vosotros/as sois, ustedes/ellos/ellas son**
Preterite (pretérito)	yo fui, tu fuiste, usted/él/ella fue, nosotros/as fuimos, vosotros/as fuisteis, ustedes/ellos/ellas fueron
Future (futuro)	yo seré, tú serás, usted/él/ella será, nosotros/as seremos, vosotros/as seréis, ustedes/ellos/ellas serán
Imperative (imperativo)	sé (tú), no seas (tú), sea (usted), seamos (nosotros/as), sed (vosotros/as), no seáis (vosotros/as), sean (ustedes)

Tener "to have" (and other verbs ending in -tener)

Present indicative	**yo tengo, tú tienes, usted/él/ella tiene, nosotros/as tenemos, vosotros/as tenéis, ustedes/ellos/ellas tienen**
Preterite (pretérito)	yo tuve, tú tuviste, usted/él/ella tuvo, nosotros/as tuvimos, vosotros/as tuvisteis, ustedes/ellos/ellas tuvieron
Future (futuro)	yo tendré, tú tendrás, usted/él/ella tendrá, nosotros/as tendremos, vosotros/as tendréis, ustedes/ellos/ellas tendrán
Imperative (imperativo)	ten tú, no tengas tú, tenga usted, tengamos nosotros/as, tened vosotros/as, no tengáis vosotros/as, tengan ustedes

Venir "to come" (including: intervenir "to intervene" and prevenir "to prevent" or "to warn")

Present indicative	**yo vengo, tú vienes, usted/él/ella viene, nosotros/as venimos, vosotros/as venís, ustedes/ellos/ellas vienen**
Preterite (pretérito)	yo vine, tú viniste, usted/él/ella vino, nosotros/as vinimos, vosotros/as vinisteis, ustedes/ellos/ellas vinieron
Future (futuro)	yo vendré, tú vendrás, usted/él/ella vendrá, nosotros/as vendremos, vosotros/as vendréis, ustedes/ellos/ellas vendrán
Imperative (imperativo)	ven (tú), no vengas (tú), venga (usted), vengamos (nosotros/as), venid (vosotros/as), no vengáis (vosotros/as), vengan (ustedes)

Ver "to see/ to view"

Present indicative	**yo veo, tú ves, usted/él/ella ve, nosotros/as vemos, vosotros/as véis, ustedes/ellos/ellas ven**
Preterite (pretérito)	yo vi, tu viste, usted/él/ella vio, nosotros/as vimos, vosotros/as visteis, ustedes/ellos/ellas vieron
Future (futuro)	yo veré, tú verás, usted/él/ella verá, nosotros/as veremos, vosotros/as veréis, ustedes/ellos/ellas verán
Imperative (imperativo)	ve tú (see), no veas tú (don't see), vea usted (see), veamos nosotros/as (let's see), ved vosotros/as (see), no veáis vosotros/as (don't see), vean ustedes (see)

Vestir "to wear" (the same patern applies for: competir "to compete", despedir "to dismiss", impeder "to prevent", medir "to measure", pedir "to order", repetir "to repeat" and server "to serve")

Present indicative	**yo visto, tú vistes, usted/él/ella viste, nosotros/as vestimos, vosotros/as vestís, ustedes/ellos/ellas visten**
Preterite (pretérito)	yo vestí, tu vestiste, usted/él/ella vistió, nosotros/as vestimos, vosotros/as vestisteis, ustedes/ellos/ellas vistieron
Future (futuro)	yo vestiré, tú vestirás, usted/él/ella vestirá, nosotros/as vestiremos, vosotros/as vestiréis, ustedes/ellos/ellas vestirán
Imperative (imperativo)	viste (tú), no vistas (tú), vista (usted), vestamos (nosotros/as), vestid (vosotros/as), no vistáis (vosotros/as), vistan (ustedes)

Volver "to return" (including: absolver "to acquit", devolver "to return", disolver "to break", desenvolver "to develop", resolver "to solve", and revolver "to stir")

Present indicative (Presente del indicativo)	**yo vuelvo, tú vuelves, usted/él/ella vuelve, nosotros/as volvemos, vosotros/as volvéis, ustedes/ellos/ellas vuelven**
Preterite	yo volví, tu volviste, usted/él/ella volvió, nosotros/as volvimos, vosotros/as volvisteis, ustedes/ellos/ellas volvieron
Future (Futuro)	yo volveré, tú volverás, usted/él/ella volverá, nosotros/as volveremos, vosotros/as volveréis, ustedes/ellos/ellas volverán
Imperative (imperativo)	vuelve (tú), no vuelvas (tú), vuelva (usted), volvamos (nosotros/as), volved (vosotros/as), no volváis (vosotros/as), vuelvan (ustedes)

This concludes our lesson on verbs. Remember that this is not a complete list. However, the patterns indicated here are true for about thousands of other Spanish verbs. Remember these patterns, especially he regular ones, and you will have mastered conjugating many other Spanish verbs not mentioned here. Enriching your vocabulary takes a little time, but becoming familiar with certain patterns in forming words is a huge step forward.

CHAPTER 10:
ADJETIVOS ESPAÑOLES (SPANISH ADJECTIVES)

Another element of a sentence that occurs almost as much as verbs is adjectives. These are words that describe or modify nouns and pronouns. They will also come in handy if you are trying to give someone a compliment or if you're asking for direction and describing a landmark.

Like other Spanish parts of speech, adjectives also have gender. The rules concerning **noun-adjective agreement** dictate that a masculine noun would require a masculine adjective. Likewise, a feminine noun also requires an adjective in the feminine gender. Most adjectives can change forms from masculine to feminine by altering its endings. Thus, the adjective *rojo* "red" can be changed to *roja* if you are modifying a feminine noun or pronoun.They can also be either singular or plural. Again, like oter parts of speech, it has to agree to the entexcedent in terms of **number and gender**.

Unlike English adjectives, Spanish ones are actually placed AFTER the noun. Well, commonly that is, but this is what constitutes the general rule. Also, it is good to remember that altering the placement of adjectives in Spanish can also alter the meaning being conveyed in the sentence.

For purposes of clarity, it would be good to note that the kinds of adjectives usually placed AFTER the noun are descriptive adjectives that are **restrictive** in nature. Meaning, they *limit* the meaning of the noun that is being modified. For example, in the phrase *la flor rosada* (the pink flower), **rosada** *(pink)* limits the meaning of the noun ***flor*** (*flower*). It indicates that you are referring to a flower of a certain color ONLY and that other flowers not belonging to the indicated category (which is *pink*) are excluded. Another example would be the phrase *la mujer española* (the Spanish woman) wherein the mention of a nationality (española) restricts the meaning of the noun *mujer*. These descriptive adjectives are usually *objective* in nature. Meaning, they describe the noun as it is and are not dependent on the tastes and peculiarities of the speaker.

As for **subjective** adjectives, as you may have already guessed, they go BEFORE the noun. This refers to those adjectives that do not necessarily limit the meaning of the noun. Rather, they seek to convey a sort of emotion or an appreciation for a quality of the noun being modified. The same is true for adjectives used to convey emphasis, as in the phrases *la blanca nieve* (the white snow) and *la oscuro noche* (the dark night). These adjectives do not, in any way, limit the meaning of the noun being modified. They are rather used to convey emphasis or certain degree of emotion and imagery to the reader.

Other adjectives that are non-descriptive in character also go before the noun. Determiners, possessive adjectives and indefinite adjectives are usually placed before the noun that they modify. Examples: *algunas manzanas* (some apples), *muchos libros* (many books), *cada persona* (each person)

Another thing, when the adjective is being further modified by an adverb (as is also common in English), the adjective is paced after the noun. For example,*Compré un anillo muy caro*(I bought a very expensive ring). The adverb *muy* (very) modifies our adjective *caro* (expensive).

How Adjective Placement can affect Meanings

We've already mentioned that Spanish adjectives can either be placed before or after the noun depending on the meaning of the sentence. Thus, it necessarily follows that there are such similar phrases that can change in meaning depending on where the adjective is being placed. An example would be the phrase *un professor viejo* and *un viejo profesor.* The former, which places the adjective after the noun, is translated as "an old/elderly teacher" whereas the latter is interpreted to mean "a long time teacher". As you may have noticed, placing the adjective before the noun makes it carry a slightly sentimental content.

Shortened Adjectives

A unique characteristic of some Spanish adjectives is that they can be shortened when placed before certain nouns. This is called "apocopation of adjectives". This happens with certain adjectives (usually non-descriptive ones) which are found before a **singular masculine** noun.

The most common example is the indefinite article *"un"* which is equivalent to the article "a" in English. It is a shortened form of *uno* "one". Thus, we say *un libro* instead of "uno libro" although the feminine form *una* is never shortened. Other examples are:
- **alguno "some"**: algún día (someday)
- **bueno "good"**: un buen hombre (a good man)
- **malo "bad"**: un mal perro (a bad dog)
- **ninguno "none"**: ningún gato (no cat)
- **primero "first"**: primer tiempo (first time)

Note that the following changes no longer apply when the noun is changed to either feminine or plural. In which case the adjectives would then revert to their original forms as in *algunas flores* (some flowers), *buena chica* (good girl) and etc.

The word *grande* "big", when placed before a noun (either masculine or feminine) is shortened to *gran*, in which case it changes in meaning and is understood as "great". Thus, *un grande día* means "a big day" while *un **gran** día* means "a great day".

Grados en Adjetivos Españoles
(Degrees in Spanish Adjectives)

Spanish adjectives, like their English equivalents, fall into three degrees: the **positive**, the **comparative**, and the **superlative**. The positive degree is used when describing only one noun or when relating one of its conditions or characteristics. For example:

- *María es hermosa.* Mary is beautiful
- *Julia es inteligente.* Julia is smart

However, there are instances when we are comparing the state of two or more nouns. Thus we might describe someone as "more beautiful" than Mary or "smarter" than Julia. Or we might say that someone is the "most beautiful" among three or more individuals.

When comparing two nouns, we use the *comparative degree* (**el grado comparative**). In Spanish, there are three ways to express the comparative degree depending on the meaning that you wish to convey:

- *más – que* (more-than)
- *menos – que* (less-than); *and*
- *tan-como* (as-as)

The first two pairs are used when comparing two nouns that are unequal in degree. Meaning, they are used to coney inequality. Thus,

- *Elena es más hermosa que María.* Elena is more beautiful than Mary.
- *Ana es menos inteligente que Julia.* Which is roughly translated as: Ana is not as smart as Julia, or something to that effect.

On the other hand, when comparing two nouns possessing a certain characteristic at the same extent, the words *tan-como* are often used. They are equivalent to the phrase "as...as" where the ellipsis is replaced by an adjective. Thus,

- *Andrea es tan hermosa como Elena.* Andrea is as beautiful as Elena.

Also, in the same way as there are words that change to form the comparative degree in English, there are also Spanish adjectives that change in form and no longer require the use of the words *más* or *menos* to convey comparison. An example in English would be the word "good" which changes to "better" when used in the comparative degree. In Spanish, the word *bueno*"good" can also be changed to *major/mejores*, meaning "better". Thus,

- *Enrique es un mejor ingeniero que yo.*Enrique is a better engineer than I (am).

Similarly, the word *malo* "bad" also has a comparative form which is *peor/peores* which means "worse".

As for the *superlative degree* (**el grado superlativo**), it is used whenever a noun is described to be the "utmost" among others in terms of a certain characteristicthat it possesses. In English, this often expressed by adding the suffix –est to an adjective, as in "best", "smartest" or "strongest".

In Spanish, this is done by using the phrase *el mas/la mas*and *el menos/la menos*. For example:

- *Ella es **la más** inteligente de todos ellos.* She is the smartest of them all.

81

- *Él es **el menos** guapo.* He is the least handsome.

The words *mejor/es* and *peor/es* (above) can also be used in the superlative degree. As in:
- *El mejor libro jamás.* The best book ever.
- *El peor president.* The worst president.

In order to tell the difference between a comparative and a superlative adjective whenever you're dealing with these two words, you'll have to rely on context. Often the word que is used in the comparative degree so that's one way to tell the difference.

Now that you know how to use Spanish adjectives, what's left is to provide a short list of the most common adjectives used in Spanish. Below I have provided some together with their corresponding antonyms. Remember (like I've always repeated before) that these words change in form according to number and gender. When you get the agreement right, you'll never go wrong.

arriba	**up**	**abajo**	**down**
dentro	right	**fuera**	left
caliente	hot	**frío**	cold
grande	big	**pequeño**	small
blanco	white	**negro**	black
limpio	clean	**sucio**	dirty
feliz	happy	**triste**	sad
alto	tall	**bajo**	short
claro	light	**obscuro/ oscuro**	dark
fuerte	strong	**débil**	weak
rápido	fast	**lento**	slow
bonito	pretty	**feo**	ugly
guapo	handsome	**feo**	ugly
simpático	kind	**antipático**	inkind

simple	simple	**complicado**	complicated
fácil	easy	**difícil**	hard
hábil	skillful	**torpe**	clumsy
amable	polite	**grosero**	rude
nuevo	new	**usado**	old/antique
joven	young	**viejo**	old
femenino	feminine	**masculino**	masculine
ganador	winner	**perdedor**	loser
cuerdo	sane	**loco**	crazy/insane
sano	well/healthy	**enfermo**	sick
seco	dry	**mujado**	wet
norte	north	**sur**	south
oriente	east	**poniente**	west
entrada	entrance	**salida**	exit
cerca	near	**lejos**	far
dulce	sweet	**agrio**	bitter
abierto	open	**cerrado**	closed
recto	straight	**curvo**	curved
presente	present	**ausente**	absent
mismo	same	**diferente**	different
bueno	good	**malo**	bad
elocuente	articulate	**inarticulado**	inarticulate
parcial	biased	**justo**	just/fair
valiente	brave	**cobarde**	cowardly
listo	ready	**desprevenido**	unprepared
fiel	faithful	**desleal/infiel**	unfaithful
gracioso	funny	**tedioso**	boring
culto	educated	**analfabeto**	illiterate
clemente	merciful	**despiadado**	ruthless
sincere/ franco	sincere	**hipócrita**	hypocritical
gordo	fat	**delgado**	thin
lleno	full	**vacío**	empty
inteligente	smart	**estúpido**	stupid/crass
bragado	energetic	**cansado**	tired

mucho	many	**poco**	few
pesado	heavy	**ligero**	light(weight)

Fifty common Spanish adjectives have been listed above. Together with their respective antonyms, that makes for a hundred adjectives altogether. ☺ Just join these elements together and you have basic Spanish at your very fingertips. Don't forget to expand that vocabulary. That's pretty much all you need in order to fully understand some basic sentences.

Learning Spanish can be a fun and rewarding experience. Aside from expanding your language horizons, you'll find out that we have a number of words in common with them and that in fact, many English words have Spanish derivatives. This could be pretty confusing at times since there are instances wherein a Spanish word would sound very similar to an English one, but there could be a slight difference in meaning. This is due to the innate dynamic character of language. Over time, words that we borrow from other languages earn a different connotation depending on how we usually use them, eventually leading them to have a different shade of meaning, if not a completely different one from the original. Take for example the word *grande* which means "big". A similar English word would be "grand" which, over time, has come to mean "great, splendid or marvelous". The proper Spanish equivalent for this would be *magníficoor grandioso*. So whenever you encounter a word that seems to be familiar, do not assume that it has the same shade of meaning as the English word that you're associating with it. It's always safer to check your dictionary. Plus you'll even learn insights on how to use the word in context. ☺ So happy reading!

CONCLUSION

Thank you again for purchasing this book!

I hope this book was able to help you to learn the basics of Spanish.

The next step is to explore more on intermediate Spanish grammar lessons and to improve your vocabulary. This is essential since the format of Spanish sentences make them easy for English speakers to understand, provided that you have a good grasp of Spanish vocabulary.

A good way to start your intermediate course would be to study the common sentence patterns, although this is something that you'll readily notice with the examples in chapter 2. Knowing how to structure your ideas will make it easier for you to convey them with confidence.

Continue this course and in due time, you'll be able to proudly boast *"Hablo español bien"*. ☺

Finally, if you enjoyed this book, then I'd like to ask you for a favor, would you be kind enough to leave a review for this book on Amazon? It'd be greatly appreciated!

Please leave a review for this book on Amazon!
http://www.amazon.com/dp/B00PLNCSAQ

Thank you and good luck!
Manuel De Cortes

PREVIEW OF:
ITALIAN FOR BEGINNERS
A Practical Guide To Learn
The Basics of Italian in 10 Days

Chapter 1 – Essential Italian Basics

It's fascinating that so many people travel the world seeing different countries, tasting the cuisine and soaking up the culture yet they fail to learn a few basic words such as *please* and *thank you*. Within the pages of this book, you will learn the basics of the Italian language. Throughout the course of this book, remember one thing: keep a steady pace and don't try to bite of more than you can chew. It is better for you to master 10 words than to tackle 50 ones that you can't recall by heart.

Italians are more responsive to foreigners that learn (and make an effort) to speak their language even if not pronounced perfectly. To them, this is a sign of respect towards them and their culture. Basic knowledge of the language – common phrases, terms and expressions – will help you feel more acquainted with the Italian customs and may even prevent unwanted [and avoidable] complications.

As you read through this book, it is highly recommended that you carry with you a recorder. As you course through the conversations and dialogues in this book, you can record yourself as you pronounce words. That way, you will be able to review your progress and listen to the way you enunciate each word and – syllable.

Some chapters contain a list of common key words and phrases that are used in everyday Italian conversations. Go through these words on a regular basis to help you memorize the words by heart. Learning a new language takes a lot of memory work. And in order to get something into your system, repetition is the key.

Articulation guide:

The Italian language is often [if not always] *pronounced as it is spelled.* There are certain rules that you must follow when it comes to pronouncing vowels and consonants. It is suggested that you read this guide before tackling words and phrases. The first column contains the vowel or consonant; the second column refers to an English word that serves as a guideline during articulation while the last column are examples of Italian words.

Note that some letters have more than one form of pronunciation. Pronunciation may change depending on the combination of letters.

Vowels	English word (To pronounce like)	Italian word
a	Math	Casa
e	Tell	Venti
	Hey	Penna
i	Pizza	Lira
o	Pot	Opera
	Port	Totale
u	Mule	Turista
Consonants	**English word**	**Italian word**
c 2 sounds: Before *e* or *i*: /ch/ Before *h, a, o* and *u*: /k/	Chocolate Chemistry	*Ciao* *Scusi*
g		

2 sounds: Before *e* or *i:* /j/ Before *h, a, o* and *u:* /g/	Geography Grass	*Gentile* *Spaghetti*
h	Always silent. Refer to consonants *c* and *g* for guidelines.	
r	Pronounced as is but should roll naturally from the tongue.	
s 2 sounds: "s" "se"	Simple Hose	*Sì* *Musica*
z 2 sounds: "ts" "tz"	Hats Tzar	*Grazie* *Zero*

Special considerations:
- Rules on pronouncing words with double consonants: Words with containing double consonants are pronounced in a similar manner except that the sound drags along for a longer period of time. There is a split second delay when saying these words whereas single consonants are pronounced continuously or fluidly.
  - **Caro - Ca<u>rr</u>o**
  - **Dona - Do<u>nn</u>a**
  - **Pala - Pa<u>ll</u>a**
- Combining letters
  There are certain rules you must observe when pronouncing letters that are combined together:
  - **ch :** /k/ - like *<u>ch</u>iaroscuro*
  - **gh :** /g/ - like *spa<u>gh</u>etti*
  - **gli :** /lli/ - like *gi<u>gl</u>i*
  - **gn :** /ñ/ - like *sauvi<u>gn</u>on*
  - **qu :** /kwa/ - like *<u>qu</u>arto*

- o **sc** – has 2 sounds
    - o Followed by **e** or **i:** /sh/ - like _sci_alle
    - o Followed by **h, a, o** or **u:** /sk/ - like _sc_olaro
- Emphasis on syllables
  Similar to the English language, stress or emphasis on particular syllables is required in order to deliver the right meaning of a particular word. Unfortunately, there is no universal rule in _Italiano_ when it comes to giving stress to a syllable of a word. This is something that you need to memorize on your own. Note that throughout this book, you will notice letters with stress symbols on the top a syllable. This serves as your guide when pronouncing words.

Tips on articulation:
You may find it quite hard to pronounce certain words at first. It can get frustrating, but you must remember to relax when you are pronouncing words. The tenser you get, the less likely you'll be able to say things properly. If a word is too "big" or complicated to pronounce, dissect it into syllables, and then determine where the emphasis should be. Enunciate slowly and then gradually gain more speed.

Keep in mind that repetition is your friend in these circumstances. Our end goal here is to be able to communicate with other so this means that you must deliver each word as clearly as possible. If you're having a hard time on pronouncing words, go over the points below:
- Listen or go over native speakers. There is a lot of audio and video material available online that is at your disposal. By listening to native speakers, you will be able to get the proper pronunciation and emphasis on particular words.
- Have a recorder on hand. When you are practicing your articulation, try to record yourself. Hearing yourself while you speak can be different from

reviewing your articulation over a voice recorder. The latter provides you with a different insight into how you communicate to a third party. Also, this helps you to compare your skills with that of a native speaker.

- If you happen to have a friend that is fluent in Italian, you can ask them to help you go over your recordings. Asking someone who is fluent in the language can give you a good constructive criticism on which points you should improve on. While you're at it, ask them to list down words that you might have mispronounced so you can focus on these.

Now that we've tackled the basics of articulation, let's have a short vocabulary lesson. Below are a few common Italian phrases. Try to pronounce each word out loud and see how it rolls on your tongue.

Buongiorno [bwon-jorno]	*Good morning* *Good day* *Good afternoon*
Buonasera [bwona-sayra]	*Good evening* *Good afternoon*
Buonanotte [bwona not-tay]	*Good night*
Arrivederci [ar-ree-vay-dayr-chee]	*Goodbye* *See you soon*
Arrivederla [ah-ree-veh-deh-rr-la]	*Goodbye* *So long* *See you soon*
Ciao [chou]	*Hello* *Hi* *So long*
Signore [see-nuor-ray]	*Sir* *Gentleman* *Lord*
Signor	*Mister*

[see-nuor]	*Mr.*
Uomo ['womo]	*Man* *Mankind*
Signora [see-nuor-ra]	*Ma'am* *Madam* *Miss* *Ms.* *Missis* *Mrs.* *Lady*
Donna [don-na]	*Woman*
Signorina [see-nuor-ree-na]	*Young lady* *Miss* *Young woman*
Sì [see]	*Of course* *Yes*
No	*No*
Per favore [per fav-o-ray]	*Please*
Grazie [grats-yay]	*Thanks* *Thank you*
Prego [pray-go]	*You're welcome* *Don't mention it!*
Prego? [pray-gó]	*Pardon?* ** (Used when you wish to have something repeated)
Scusi [scoos-ee]	*Excuse me* *I am sorry* **(Can also be used in order to call someone's attention)
Mi dispiace [me dis-pee-arch-ay]	*I beg your pardon* *I am [very] sorry*
Come sta? [komay sta]	*How are you?* *How are you doing?*

Bene, grazie [bay-nay, grat-see]	*Well, thank you!*
E Lei? [ay lay]	*And you?* *And how about you?*
Molto bene, grazie [molto bay-nay grats-yay]	*Very well, thank you!*
Non troppo bene [non tropeu bay-nay]	*Not too well...*
Non ćè male [non ke meil] ****(ćè** = the combination of letters is pronounced as "che")	*Not too bad / Not that bad...*
Parlare [par'lare]	*To speak* *To talk (a lot)* *To chatter*
Parla inglese/italiano? [par-la]	*Do you speak English* *Do you speak Italian?*
Parli più lentamente [par-li piu len-ta-mente]	*To speak more gradually* *To speak slowly*
Va bene [va bay-nay]	*Okay* *That's okay* *Alright* *Certainly*

Now that you know a few common phrases, try to repeat them about 15-20 times over. If you are recording yourself, try to review how you pronounce and which syllables you put stress on. Be cautious of how you deliver your words.

Practice conversations and dialogues (Dialoghi)
Below are three conversations to help you practice rudimentary Italian conversation. Play both parts and try to visualize having a conversation with a native speaker. If you

wish to make the scenario more realistic, have a native speaker help you practice these dialogues.

- Dialogue 1: Common greeting.
  Signor Francesco: *Buongiorno, signora Moretti!*
  Signora Moretti: *Buongiorno, signor Francesco. Come sta?*
  Signor Francesco: *Molto bene, grazie. E lei?*
  Signora Moretti: *Bene. Arrivederci signor!*
  Signor Francesco: *Arrivederci.*
- Dialogue 2: Asking if a person speaks English
  Mr. Smith: *Buongiorno, signore! Parla inglese?*
  Signor Malta: *Buongiorno, signore! Sì, molto bene.*

Quick tips on syntax and proper use of words:

- When greeting someone...
  - o **Buongiorno** – is used until 4 in the afternoon during the summer season; just before dark during the winter.
  - o **Buonasera** – used after *Buongiorno* when it is already dark.
  - o **Buonanotte** – used when one is going to bed or when it is time to call it a night.

- When bidding someone goodbye...
  - o **Arrivederci** – used when saying goodbye to someone you plan to see again soon; used also when leaving a place of business.
  - o **Arrivederla** – a more formal expression. Used when talking to someone of a high position or in a professional situation.
  - o **Ciao** – has a double meaning of *hello* and *goodbye*; only used in an informal or casual setting; never in a formal or professional scenario.

- Appropriate titles: addressing yourself and others
  - **Signor** is the direct equivalent of *Mister/ Mr.* in the English language hence it should always be followed by a surname.
  - **Signore** is used when the name of the person you are speaking to is unknown.
  - The same applies for women with the use of **Signora; signorina.** Note that the former is used to address older or adult women whereas the latter is used to address unmarried and young women.

- How to properly and politely ask a question
  Similar to the English language, when asking a question you must place the proper intonation at the end of your sentence or phrase to indicate that you are making a query. The same goes with writing.

Practice situations:
See how well you apply the lessons that have just been tackled in this chapter. Use the appropriate greeting/ term/ word for the situations given below.

1. Provide the appropriate greeting for the following:
   a. 8:00
   b. 16:00
   c. 19:00
   d. Bedtime
2. A vendor in a boutique has offered to sell you a trinket but you are not interested.
   a. *No*
   b. *Per favore*
   c. *Mi dispiace*
   d. *No, grazie*
3. You wish to call the attention of someone.
4. How do you respond when someone thanks you?

5. You've just ended a dinner party with friend. How do you say goodbye?
6. You'd like to ask a friend for a favor, how do you begin your sentence?
7. You accidentally bumped into a stranger. How do you make an apology?
8. You bumped into an acquaintance and they have asked you how you have been. How do you ask how he's doing?
9. You walk into a boutique and you would like to know if they shopkeeper speaks English. What do you ask him?
10. Someone has been explaining directions to you but you did not understand. How do you ask them politely to speak slowly and repeat the instructions?

Answer key:
1. & b. *Buongiorno*; c. *Buonasera*; d. *Buonanotte*
2. *No, grazie*
3. *Scusi*
4. *prego*
5. *Ciao*
6. *Per favore*
7. *Mi dispiace*
8. *Molto bene, grazie... Come sta?*
9. *Buongiorno / Buonasera, parla Inglese?*
10. *Scusi / Prego? Parli più lentamente*

CHECK OUT MY OTHER BOOKS

Below you'll find some of my other popular books that are popular on Amazon and Kindle as well. Simply click on the links below to check them out. Alternatively, you can visit my author page on Amazon to see other work done by me.

1) *Italian For Beginners: A practical guide to learn the basics of Italian in 10 days*
   http://www.amazon.com/dp/B00Q5B49XM
2) *French For Beginners: A practical guide to learn the basics of French in 10 days*
   http://www.amazon.com/dp/B00TIVX7CU
3) *Italy Travel Guide: Top 40 Place You Can't Miss!*
   http://www.amazon.com/dp/B00M7V7PNA

CPSIA information can be obtained at www.ICGtesting.com
Printed in the USA
LVOW06s0034190815

450607LV00030B/950/P